Those were the days ...

Endurance racing at Silverstone
in the 1970s & 1980s

VELOCE

Other great books from Veloce –

Those Were The Days ... Series
Alpine Trials & Rallies 1910-1973 (Pfundner)
American 'Independent' Automakers – AMC to Willys 1945 to 1960 (Mort)
American Station Wagons – The Golden Era 1950-1975 (Mort)
American Trucks of the 1950s (Mort)
American Trucks of the 1960s (Mort)
American Woodies 1928-1953 (Mort)
Anglo-American Cars from the 1930s to the 1970s (Mort)
Austerity Motoring (Bobbitt)
Austins, The last real (Peck)
Brighton National Speed Trials (Gardiner)
British Lorries of the 1950s (Bobbitt)
British Lorries of the 1960s (Bobbitt)
British Touring Car Racing (Collins)
British Police Cars (Walker)
British Woodies (Peck)
Café Racer Phenomenon, The (Walker)
Dune Buggy Phenomenon, The (Hale)
Dune Buggy Phenomenon Volume 2, The (Hale)
Endurance Racing at Silverstone in the 1970s & 1980s (Parker)
Hot Rod & Stock Car Racing in Britain in the 1980s (Neil)
Last Real Austins 1946-1959, The (Peck)
MG's Abingdon Factory (Moylan)
Motor Racing at Brands Hatch in the Seventies (Parker)
Motor Racing at Brands Hatch in the Eighties (Parker)
Motor Racing at Crystal Palace (Collins)
Motor Racing at Goodwood in the Sixties (Gardiner)
Motor Racing at Nassau in the 1950s & 1960s (O'Neil)
Motor Racing at Oulton Park in the 1960s (McFadyen)
Motor Racing at Oulton Park in the 1970s (McFadyen)
Superprix – The Story of Birmingham Motor Race (Page & Collins)
Three Wheelers (Bobbitt)

General motorsport
Alpine & Renault – The Development of the Revolutionary Turbo F1 Car 1968 to 1979 (Smith)
Alpine & Renault – The Sports Prototypes 1963 to 1969 (Smith)
Alpine & Renault – The Sports Prototypes 1973 to 1978 (Smith)
Anatomy of the Works Minis (Moylan)
Autodrome (Collins & Ireland)
Autodrome 2 (Collins & Ireland)
Bahamas Speed Weeks, The (O'Neil)
BMC Competitions Department Secrets (Turner)
British at Indianapolis, The (Wagstaff)
BRM – A Mechanic's Tale (Salmon)
BRM V16 (Ludvigsen)
Cliff Allison, The Official Biography of – From the Fells to Ferrari – (Gauld)
Coventry Climax Racing Engines (Hammill)
Daily Mirror 1970 World Cup Rally 40, The (Robson)
Fast Ladies – Female Racing Drivers 1888 to 1970 (Bouzanquet)
Ferrari 288 GTO, The Book of the (Sackey)
Formula 5000 Motor Racing, Back then ... and back now (Lawson)
Forza Minardi! (Vigar)
GT – The World's Best GT Cars 1953-73 (Dawson)
Hillclimbing & Sprinting – The Essential Manual (Short & Wilkinson)
Jack Sears, The Official Biography of – Gentleman Jack (Gauld)
Jaguar, The Rise of (Price)
Jaguar XJ 220 – The Inside Story (Moreton)
Jaguar XJ-S (Long)
John Chatham – 'Mr Big Healey' – The Official Biography (Burr)
Lola – The Illustrated History (1957-1977) (Starkey)
Lola – All the Sports Racing & Single-seater Racing Cars 1978-1997 (Starkey)
Lola T70 – The Racing History & Individual Chassis Record 4th Edition (Starkey)
Lotus 49 (Oliver)
Maximum Mini (Booij)
Mini Cooper – The Real Thing! (Tipler)
Montlhéry, The Story of the Paris Autodrome (Boddy)
Motor Racing – Reflections of a Lost Era (Carter)
Motorsport In colour, 1950s (Wainwright)
Northeast American Sports Car Races 1950-1959 (O'Neil)
Speedway – Auto racing's ghost tracks (Collins & Ireland)
Tales from the Toolbox (Oliver)
Toleman Story, The (Hilton)
Unraced (Collins)
Works Minis, The Last (Purves & Brenchley)

From Veloce Publishing's new imprints:

Battle Cry!
Soviet General & field rank officer uniforms: 1955 to 1991 (Streather)
Red & Soviet military & paramilitary services: female uniforms 1941-1991 (Streather)

Hubble & Hattie
Complete Dog Massage Manual, The – Gentle Dog Care (Robertson)
Dinner with Rover (Paton-Ayre)
Dog Games – Stimulating play to entertain your dog and you (Blenski)
Dog Relax – Relaxed dogs, relaxed owners (Pilguj)
Know Your Dog – The guide to a beautiful relationship (Birmelin)
My dog is blind – but lives life to the full! (Horsky)
Smellorama – nose games for dogs (Theby)
Waggy Tails & Wheelchairs (Epp)
Winston ... the dog who changed my life (Klute)
You and Your Border Terrier – The Essential Guide (Alderton)
You and Your Cockapoo – The Essential Guide (Alderton)

www.veloce.co.uk

First published in May 2010 by Veloce Publishing Limited, Veloce House, Parkway Farm Business Park, Middle Farm Way, Poundbury, Dorchester, Dorset, DT1 3AR, England. Fax 01305 250479/e-mail info@veloce.co.uk/web www.veloce.co.uk or www.velocebooks.com.
ISBN: 978-1-845842-77-2 UPC: 6-36847-04277-6
© Chas Parker and Veloce Publishing 2010. All rights reserved. With the exception of quoting brief passages for the purpose of review, no part of this publication may be recorded, reproduced or transmitted by any means, including photocopying, without the written permission of Veloce Publishing Ltd. Throughout this book logos, model names and designations, etc, have been used for the purposes of identification, illustration and decoration. Such names are the property of the trademark holder as this is not an official publication.
Readers with ideas for automotive books, or books on other transport or related hobby subjects, are invited to write to the editorial director of Veloce Publishing at the above address.
British Library Cataloguing in Publication Data – A catalogue record for this book is available from the British Library. Typesetting, design and page make-up all by Veloce Publishing Ltd on Apple Mac. Printed in India by Replika Press.

Contents

Acknowledgements & bibliography 4
Foreword 5
Introduction 7
1976 9
1977 16
1978 18
1979 24
1980 32
1981 39
1982 45
1983 50
1984 56
1985 61
1986 68
1987 74
1988 80
Results 85
Index 95

Dedication

To Jon and Will

Acknowledgements

Thanks to Kevin Wood and Tim Wright at LAT for access to bound volumes of *Autosport* and for the photographs on page 17. All other photographs are the author's own.

Thanks also to Stephanie Sykes at the BRDC for permission to reproduce Silverstone programme covers and maps.

Bibliography

Sundry copies of *Autosport*, 1976-1988

Silverstone 6-Hour and 1000km race programmes, 1976-1988, published by Silverstone Circuits Ltd

Pole Position, celebrating the Diamond Jubilee of the British Racing Drivers' Club, published by the BRDC, 1987

British Grand Prix, Maurice Hamilton, published by The Crowood Press, 1989

World Sportscar Championship DVD Reviews 1983, 1984, 1985, 1986, 1987, 1988, published by Duke Video, 2009

www.racingsportscars.com

www.wspr-racing.com

Foreword

The accounts of the races in this book are not intended to be definitive reports, but more a general overview of what happened and my impressions of the events, albeit as best as I can recall from over 20 years on. Some of them I remember clearly; others, I confess, are a bit of a blur. But, by looking back at the photos and reading contemporary reports, I've managed to jog my memory enough to fill in the gaps.

I usually kissed goodbye to a couple of rolls of 36 exposure colour transparency film at long meetings like these, and the hardest part of compiling this book has been selecting a few photos from the many hundred I accumulated over the years. In the selection process, I have tried to illustrate the wide variety of cars that used to contest these events.

I started going to endurance races in 1970, and fell in love with long-distance sports car racing. I attended the BOAC 1000km world championship events at Brands Hatch from 1970-72, and the British Airways 1000km in 1974, but was disappointed that there was no championship round in this country in either 1973 or 1975.

So I was pleased when a long-distance event was scheduled on the calendar at Silverstone in May 1976. Four of us travelled up in my 850cc Mini from the south coast, a journey which took around four hours each way since you had to go through the centre of London. There was no M25 in those days.

Some people find endurance racing boring. Cars slogging their way round and round a track for hours on end and the field strung out with competitors sometimes many laps apart, meaning there's rarely any close dicing for position, and making it hard to keep track of what's happening and who's where half the time. In fact, the term 'endurance' can sometimes apply to the poor spectator as well as the competitor!

But I loved it. I enjoyed walking around a circuit, watching from different vantage points, soaking up the atmosphere, going off and looking round the shops or paddock and coming back to see what had changed. It was a much more relaxed affair than a Grand Prix or other major race, but somehow held the same kudos for me. These were, after all, the same cars and drivers that battled it out day and night at the most famous motor race in the world, the Le Mans 24-Hours.

The following year, 1977, Britain had two rounds of the championship, one at Silverstone and the other at Brands. I chose to go to the latter because it was nearer, but I've always regretted not being at that '77 Silverstone event, simply because it left a gap in my CV for endurance racing. Apart from that one miss, I attended all of the 6-Hour and 1000km events at the circuit throughout the late seventies and eighties, during what became a golden age of endurance sports car racing, the Group C era.

And the race itself became something of a classic, as well. The fact that it immediately preceded Le Mans on the world endurance calendar meant that many teams used it as a shakedown test for the most important event of the year, and in the early days new cars would make their racing debuts there – the long-tailed Porsche 935 'Moby Dick' for example, or the Dome from Japan.

I saw Jaguar score its first victory in 29 years there in 1986, repeating the feat for the next two years before going on to take a historic victory at Le Mans in 1988. I always used to head for parc fermé, on the inside of Woodcote, at the end of the race. Each car would be ushered into this collecting area by the marshals, and the drivers would emerge tired and sweating from the sauna that was the inside of a cramped, usually enclosed, endurance racer.

As endurance racing waned in the late '80s, so too did the Silverstone event, until in 1989 Britain's round of the endurance championship was held at Donington Park. I didn't go. Silverstone hosted a round of the German Sports Car Championship for similar cars that year, but it was a sprint event with a small entry. I didn't go to that either.

The event did return in 1990-92 as a shorter 500km 'sprint' race, and as a one-off American Le Mans Series race in 2000. It now lives on in the form of a 1000km round of the Le Mans Endurance Series, which has been held since 2004.

But it was that period from 1976 to 1988 that, to me, was the most memorable. A spring day at Silverstone, with a whole six hours or so of racing ahead of you and time to take it all in.

Chas Parker

Introduction

Silverstone started life in 1943 as a World War II bomber airfield, and became the base for the RAF's 17th Operational Training Unit, where aircrew were instructed in flying Wellington bombers. One of the lesser known facts about the place is that the astronomer Patrick Moore trained as a bomber pilot there.

After the war, in 1947, a group of local enthusiasts held an unofficial race using the runways, and the Royal Automobile Club, which had been looking for a new motor sport venue since the pre-war circuits of Brooklands and Donington were unusable, took out a lease on the airfield in 1948.

By using a combination of the perimeter road and runways, it was possible to lay out a 3.67 mile track using straw bales and oil drums. The start line, in those days, was between Abbey Curve and Woodcote, the corners being named mainly after local landmarks. Abbey referred to Luffield Abbey Farm, near the site of the ancient Luffield Abbey, although Woodcote was named after the RAC's country club at Woodcote Park in Surrey. Copse referred to the nearby Seven Copses Wood, Maggots was named after nearby Maggots Moor, and Becketts and Chapel after the ruins of Thomas à Beckett Chapel. Hangar Straight referred to two large aircraft hangers, and Stowe was named after the nearby Stowe School. The

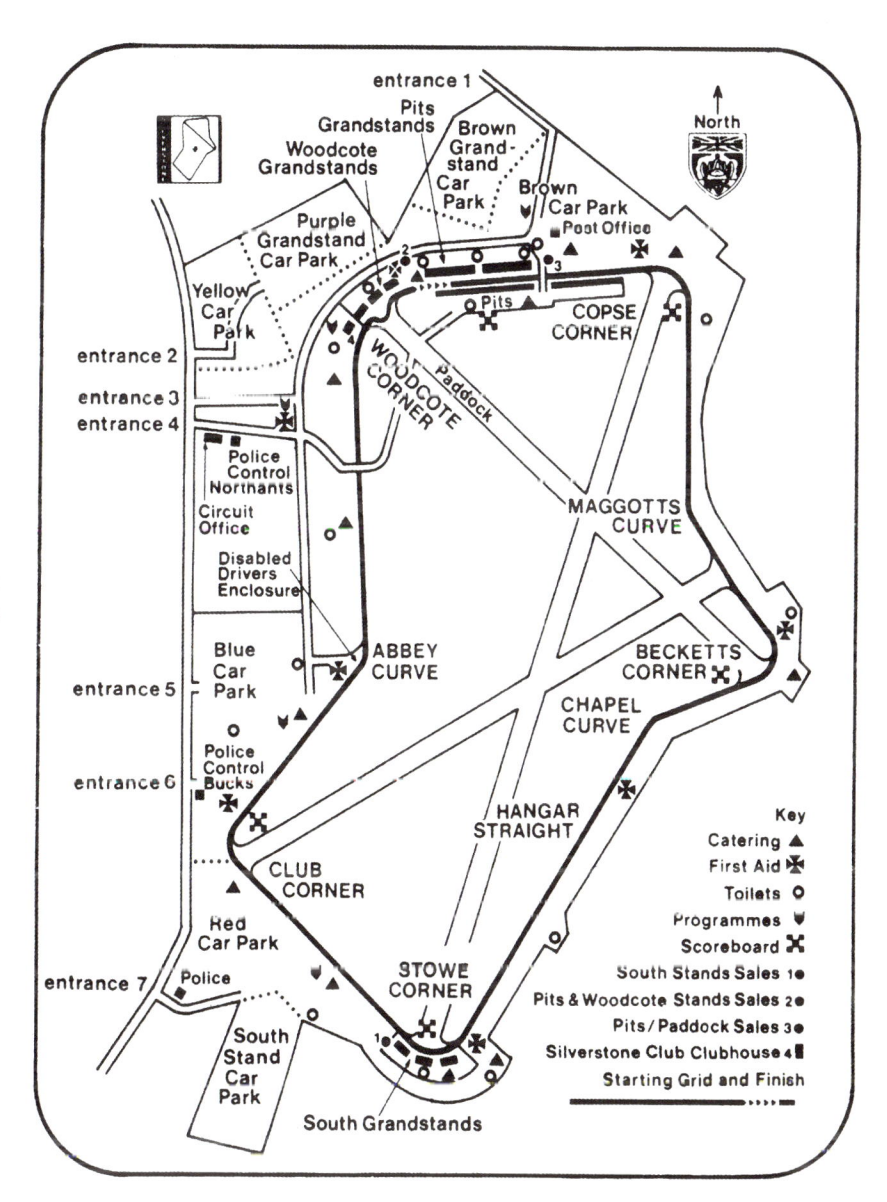

Map of the 1976 circuit. (Reproduced with permission from the BRDC)

Silverstone
The Home of British Motor Racing for 40 years

Royal Automobile Club in Pall Mall gave Club Corner its name, and the two infield straights along the runways were named after British drivers, Dick Seaman and Henry Segrave.

The first event held at Silverstone was the 1948 RAC Grand Prix, which drew a crowd of 100,000 to watch the top drivers of the day compete in the first major motor sport event in the country for ten years. The race was won by Luigi Villoresi, driving a Maserati.

In 1949 the track was revised. Abandoning the runways and using only the perimeter roads, with a tight chicane at Club Corner, it adopted a general layout that was to remain largely unchanged for 25 years. In 1952, the start line was moved to its present location, between Woodcote and Copse, and in 1975 a chicane was installed at Woodcote to reduce the speed of the cars over the start-finish line. This circuit configuration was in use for the majority of the time covered by this book. In 1987, a new tight left-right dog-leg between Abbey and Woodcote was introduced to further reduce speeds.

Silverstone is known as 'The Home of British Motor Racing' and for a while it was also the home of some wonderful endurance racing, which is what this book is all about.

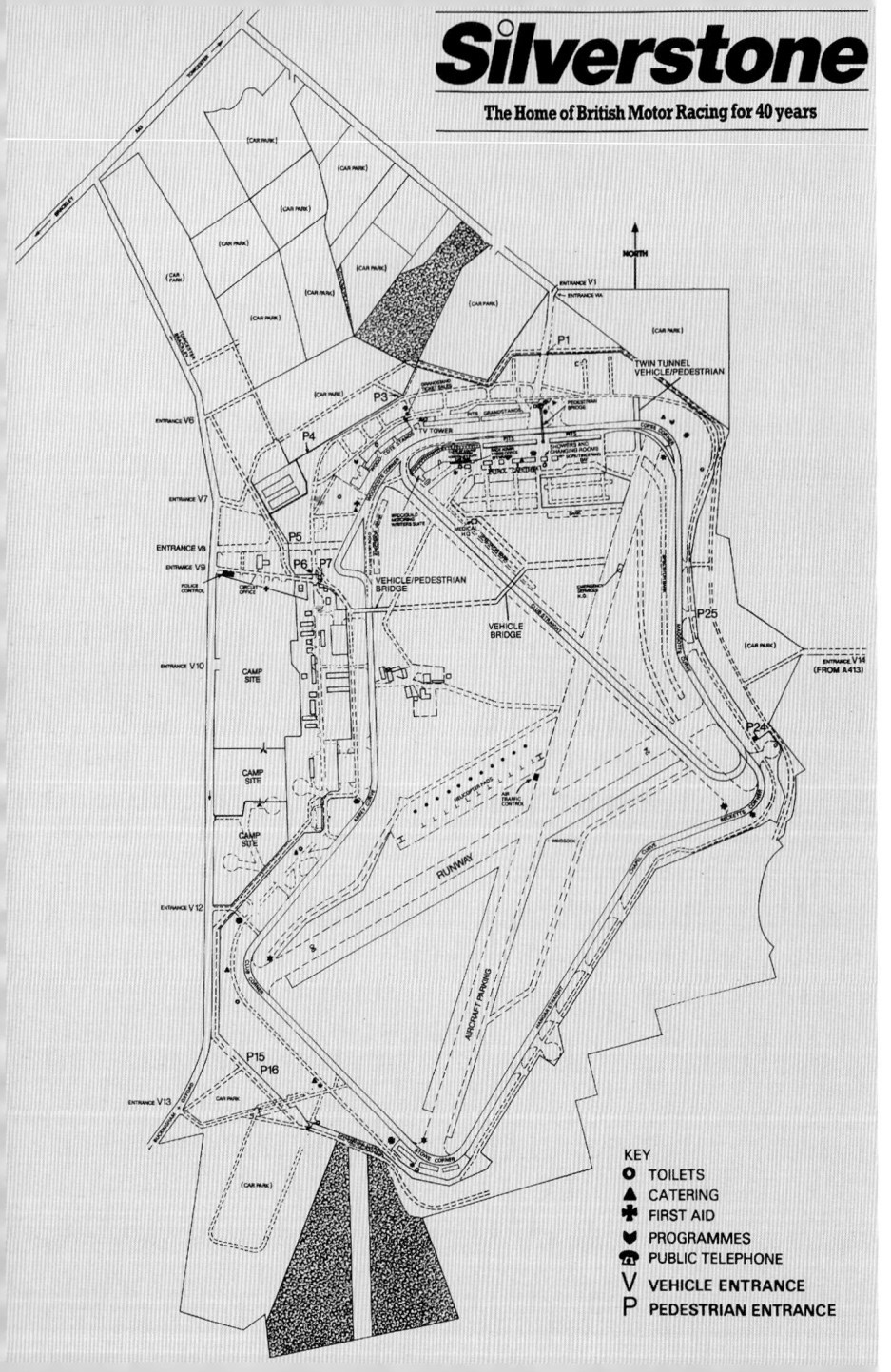

Map of the 1988 circuit. (Reproduced with permission from the BRDC)

1976

Sunday 9 May 1976 was one of those days you never forget. The Silverstone 6-Hours was the third round of that year's World Championship for Manufacturers and the only one to be held in Britain. Endurance racing had been split into two categories – Group 5 and Group 6. The former, which this race was for, was known as 'Silhouette' racing, since outwardly the cars bore some resemblance to road-going tourers whereas, under the skin, they were very different beasts indeed. Group 6, on the other hand, was for out-and-out sports prototypes and ran in a separate championship, no round of which was held in the UK that year.

The Group 5 category produced some of the most powerful touring cars to be seen and attracted top class teams and drivers including, to this round at least, one former and four current Grand Prix drivers.

The field was split into three classes, the top one being for cars of 3001-6000cc which included BMW 3.5 CSLs, Porsche 935s and even an MGB GT V8. Below that, Class B catered for engine sizes of 2001-3000cc (Porsche Carrera RSRs and a rotary-engined Mazda RX3), while Class C was for cars of up to 2000cc, which in this case meant Ford Escorts and a Toyota Celica.

A total of only 18 cars lined up on the grid from an original entry of 27. Not very impressive when you consider that there was six hours of racing ahead and natural attrition was going to account for some of the runners. But at least the cars in the first front rows looked absolutely gorgeous, and none more so than the pole-sitting Martini Porsche of Jochen Mass and Jacky Ickx. Alongside it on the front row was another eye-catching machine – the BMW 3.5 CSL Turbo –

1976 race programme.
(Reproduced with permission from the BRDC)

piloted by Ronnie Peterson and Gunnar Nilsson. Behind them sat two more Porsches: the Kremer-entered 935 of Bob Wollek and Hans Heyer, and the Carrera RSR of entrants Egon Evertz and Leo Kinnunen.

On row three was a pair of BMW 3.5 CSLs: Dieter Quester and Albrecht Krebs in a Schnitzer-entered car, and Harald Grohs and Sam Posey in the Alpina entry.

The Kremer Porsche 935 of Bob Wollek and Han Heyer sits in the Silverstone pit lane. The car would eventually finish just 1.18 seconds behind the winning BMW 3.5 CSL after a thrilling battle.

The new works Martini Porsche 935 looked splendid during the morning's pit road walkabout.

The MGB GT V8 of Bob Neville and Derek Worthington – which finished eighth in the race – is fuelled in the pits prior to the start.

Behind them lurked another BMW 3.5 CSL, entered by Hermetite Racing with the British pairing of Tom Walkinshaw and John Fitzpatrick on board. The car had qualified badly as it was hampered by a misfire that wasn't rectified until the night before the race. Alongside them was a 2-litre Jolly Club Ford Escort driven by Italians Umberto Grano and Martino Finotto.

The cars lined up on Sunday morning for the midday start. The flag dropped and the field surged towards Copse Corner. Except for the pole position car of Jacky Ickx, that is, whose clutch disintegrated as he changed up into third gear. The fastest car on the track crawled slowly round as far as Becketts before Ickx pulled over. The crowd groaned.

This left Ronnie Peterson's BMW in the lead, followed by the similar car of Dieter Quester, the Porsche of Bob Wollek, John Fitzpatrick's BMW, Leo Kinnunen's Porsche and Harald Groh's BMW. These six were already pulling out a gap from the rest of the field, which was led by the Toyota Celica of Manfred Schurti.

Meanwhile, back up at Becketts, the Porsche mechanics were shouting instructions to Ickx to try and get the Martini car moving again, outside assistance not being allowed. Eventually they gave up and, instead, Ickx,

John Fitzpatrick in the victorious Hermetite BMW 3.5 CSL that he shared with Tom Walkinshaw. After six hours of racing, the car was just 1.18 seconds ahead of the second-placed Porsche at the flag.

Dieter Quester in the Schnitzer-entered BMW 3.5 CSL, which was co-driven by Albrecht Krebs. The pair led the race for a while, but eventually retired with a blown engine.

Ronnie Peterson, in the works turbocharged BMW 3.5 CSL he co-drove with Gunnar Nilsson, was the early star of the race, but retired with gearbox problems after just 43 laps.

who had by now been joined by Mass, began to push the stricken car down Silverstone's Club Straight and back to the pits.

Peterson and Wollek slowly began to pull away until, only half-an-hour into the race, Peterson pitted for new tyres. He dropped down the field but immediately began a superb chase, eventually working his way back up to second and keeping the crowd well entertained. At the end of the first hour Wollek led from Peterson, with Quester, Fitzpatrick, Evertz and Finotto all a lap behind. Not long afterwards, though, Peterson crawled into the pits with third and fifth gears missing. The car had been spectacular while it had lasted, but its race was over after just 43 laps.

However, as one front-runner retired, so another was about to return. In the Porsche pits mechanics had removed the engine from the Ickx/Mass car in just 12 minutes, but it took another 20 to remove the gearbox in order to access the clutch. Finally, an hour-and-three-quarters after the event had started, the Martini-liveried car stormed back into the race, much to the delight of the crowd. They had no hopes of winning, but they were going to put on a good show and go for fastest lap.

The next car to hit problems was the leading 935 of Wollek. He had pitted on the two-hour mark but stuttered to a halt, smoke pouring from the car, as he tried to pull away. The problem was a broken turbo axle that mechanics were able to fix in just 15 minutes, but it dropped him to fourth place, behind the Krebs BMW, Walkinshaw's BMW and Kinnunen's Porsche.

Soon after, the Hermetite BMW stopped to change brake pads, dropping out of the lead battle, which was

13

Endurance racing at Silverstone in the 1970s & 1980s

After losing an hour-and-three-quarters having its clutch replaced, the Martini Porsche 935 turbo of Jacky Ickx and Jochen Mass finally re-joined the race, setting the fastest lap on its way to tenth place.

getting interesting. The Evertz/Kinnunen Carrera RSR, with Evertz at the wheel, had been gaining on the lead BMW, now driven by Dieter Quester, and passed him with two-and-a-half-hours run. Not long after, however, the Porsche lost time at a pit stop and, at the halfway point, the BMW was back in front, the Hermetite Walkinshaw/Fitzpatrick car was back up to second – albeit a lap adrift – with the chasing Porsche a further two laps behind.

An hour-and-a-half later, the leading BMW of Krebs and Quester suffered a blown engine, leaving Evertz and Kinnunen two laps ahead of Fitzpatrick, whose co-driver, Walkinshaw, had left the event to fly to Thruxton and compete in a British Touring Car race! Behind them was the Wollek/Heyer Porsche, a further lap adrift.

By the five-hour mark Fitzpatrick, who had been driving the wheels off the Hermetite BMW, had closed right up on the leader, though was still a lap down. A few minutes later Kinnunen pitted, handing the lead to Fitzpatrick, until *he* did the same the following lap. While Fitzpatrick was stationery, the Wollek/Heyer Porsche, with Heyer at the wheel, took the lead. This was gripping stuff and, with three-quarters-of-an-hour to go, all three cars were on the same lap ...

1976

Harald Grohs, partnered by Hughes de Fierlandt, took the Alpina BMW 3.5 CSL to an eventual fourth place.

Half-an-hour to go and Fitzpatrick had closed on Kinnunen and passed him, as did Heyer, who was also closing on the BMW. The gap kept coming down until, finally, the Porsche swept past on Hanger Straight with just 15 minutes left to run. The crowd – which had been hoping for a 'home' victory – groaned. A few minutes later, though, the lead Porsche stormed into the pits for a final 'splash and dash' refuelling, rejoining the track 24 seconds adrift of the BMW and with nine minutes left. The gap kept coming down as the minutes ticked away. We looked at our watches, willing the clock to reach 6.00pm, but the pair crossed the line with 15 seconds left to run – they would have to do another lap. Our hearts were in our mouths and I'd never felt such excitement at the end of a motor race, let alone one of six-hours endurance.

Round they came for the final time and, to the cheers of the delighted and excited crowd, Fitzpatrick just held off the charging Heyer to take victory by 1.18 seconds. Tom Walkinshaw had a doubly successful day as he also won the Thruxton Touring Car Championship race in a Ford Capri, while Ickx and Mass achieved their objective of setting fastest lap, eventually finishing in tenth place.

1977

I'm ashamed to admit that I didn't attend the 1977 Silverstone 6-Hours. It was the only one I missed in 13 years, though. For the sake of completeness, I am including a brief resumé of the race here.

The meeting was dominated by the works Martini Porsche 935-77 of Jacky Ickx and Jochen Mass, making up for their disappointment from the previous year.

The first few rows of the grid were comprised entirely of Porsches, with the works car on pole and Bob Wollek/John Fitzpatrick in a Kremer-entered 935 alongside. Behind them came another four 935s before the BMW 320i of Ronnie Peterson and Helmut Kelleners, which was in seventh place. The rest of the grid was made up of 934 and Carrera Porsches, Ford Escorts and Capris, a couple of Datsuns and an Aston Martin V8.

Mass shot-away at the start and quickly opened up a lead. Behind him, the Wollek/Fitzpatrick car and the Gelo example of Rolf Stommelen/Toine Hezemans fought over second place – Stommelen at one point hitting one of the famous Silverstone hares, damaging the front spoiler and brake duct.

But it was the Peterson/Kelleners BMW that was keeping the crowd entertained, the Swede sliding the car through the corners on the way to an eventual class victory.

Up front, the works car maintained its advantage during the first half of the race, but began to suffer from excessive brake pad wear. A long pit stop in the fifth-hour allowed the Wollek/Fitzpatrick car to take the lead, until its own stop; a situation which repeated itself when the Martini car made its last scheduled fuel stop in the final hour.

1977 race programme.
(Reproduced with permission from the BRDC)

Then, with less than 30 minutes to go, it started to rain. Fitzpatrick was the first to pit for rain tyres, resuming two laps in arrears but taking over seven seconds a lap off the leading car driven by Jochen Mass, who didn't come in for another three laps. A botched pit stop would have lost Mass the race but, as it was, the German resumed still a lap ahead.

And that's how it stayed to the end. Third was the Stommelen/Hezemans car, which had battled for a long time with the Jolly Club-entered 935 of Martino Finotto and Carlo Facetti, until the latter suffered suspension problems and dropped back to sixth.

Peterson brought the BMW home in fourth, continuing his crowd-pleasing activities by staying out in the rain on slick tyres to take the 2 litre class win.

It sounds like it was a good race, and I wish I'd been there.

Top: Pit stop for the winning Martini Porsche 935-77 of Jacky Ickx and Jochen Mass. (Photo: LAT)

Bottom: Ronnie Peterson entertained the crowd in the BMW 320i he shared with Helmut Kelleners, eventually finishing fourth. (Photo: LAT)

1978

Some cars you just fall in love with as soon as you see them. That's the way it was with Porsche's glorious 1978 incarnation of its hugely successful 935 model. The long-tailed car made its debut at Silverstone and was dubbed the 935-78, although it came to be known as 'Moby Dick,' and it just destroyed the opposition.

The car was driven by the usual pairing of Jacky Ickx and Jochen Mass, who put it on pole position.

In those days, a number of privateer teams also ran Porsche 935s, albeit without the latest bodywork of the works car. Sharing the front row with the works team was the Gelo Racing Porsche 935-77 of John Fitzpatrick and Toine Hezemans. Behind them, the Kremer 935-77 of Bob Wollek and Henri Pescarolo, and the second Gelo car of Derek Bell, Hans Heyer and Klaus Ludwig completed the second row.

Just to confuse spectators, drivers often qualified more than one car within a team, thereby enabling them to be swapped around during the race if necessary. Thus, on row three, we had the combination of Hezemans, Heyer and Fitzpatrick to drive a third Gelo 935-77, with the first non-Porsche on the grid – the BMW 320T of Ronnie Peterson and Hans Stuck – sat alongside it. Behind them, lay a plethora of more Porsches (935s, 934s and a 924) and BMWs, with just a single Lotus Elan and Ford Capri to add interest.

The entry was split into two classes – up to 2-litre and over 2-litre, with the bulk of the field coming from the latter category. Within these were other classifications: Group 5 Special Production cars; Group 4 Grand Touring cars; Group 3 Series Production Grand Touring cars; Group 2 Touring Cars and Group 1 Series

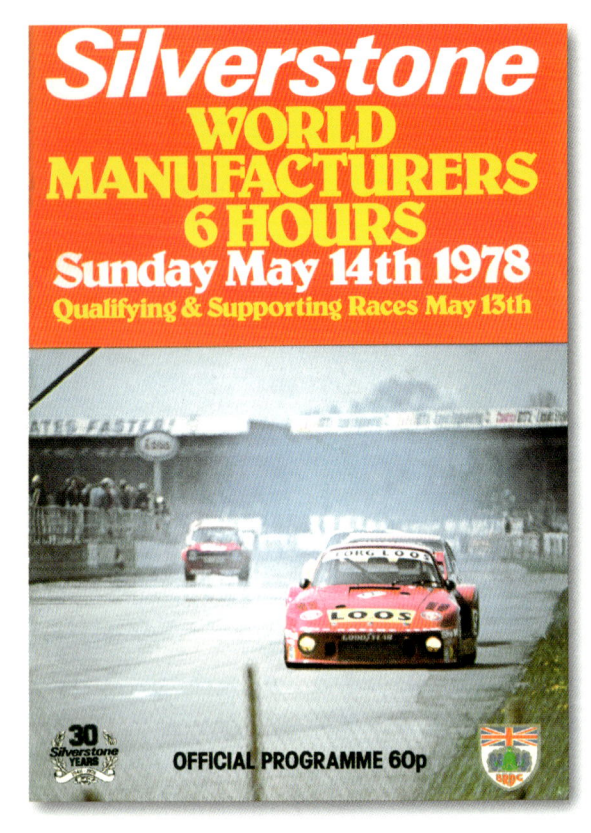

1978 race programme.
(Reproduced with permission from the BRDC)

Production Touring cars. It was easier to think of them as up to and over 2-litre though.

There had been light rain just before the 27-strong field lined up for the midday start, but things were looking brighter as they set off, with Mass immediately taking the initiative from Hezemans. At the end of the first lap, these two led from Fitzpatrick, Wollek, Ludwig,

Freddy Kottulinsky and Markus Hotz took their BMW 320i to fourth place overall and second in the up to 2-litre class.

Claude Haldi in a Meccarillos Racing 935, up from tenth on the grid, and Peterson in the BMW.

Mass continued to pull away, and it soon became clear that, barring unforeseen incidents, the works Porsche was going to run out an easy winner. Having one car or driver dominate an event can be dull, but there is also something magnificent in excellence – in seeing something honed to perfection, driven with skill, and leaving all others in its wake. So it was that day.

With the sun coming out, teams started to head for the pits for dry tyres. Wollek pitted first, but Mass in the Martini car waited as long as possible before making his stop. Mass was far enough ahead of the second placed car to be able to make a 42 second stop and still rejoin in the lead. After an hour, Mass led from Wollek, whose early stop had leap-frogged him ahead of Fitzpatrick, who then dropped to fourth after a delay in the pits. In third was the Ludwig/Bell Gelo car, while the Peterson/Stuck BMW held on to fifth.

The light rain returned after a while – which is always a nuisance when you're halfway round walking the circuit and there's little cover to be had. No matter, it was quite entertaining – a number of cars getting caught out and ending up in the catch-fencing. The Wollek/Pescarolo car made the mistake of changing to wet tyres at this point as it was soon back in when the track began to dry again, thus losing the early advantage. Providing more entertainment were Peterson and Stuck

The works Martini Porsche 935-78, dubbed 'Moby Dick,' attracted a lot of interest during the pit road walkabout.

Ronnie Peterson and Hans Stuck ran as high as second in their works BMW 320T, but eventually retired after four hours with transmission problems.

in the BMW – both drivers pushing the car to its limit – and by the halfway point in the race they had worked their way up to second place.

Just prior to this, a fire in the pits involving the Klaus Drees/Mike Franey Porsche 935 had caused a bit of excitement. Fuel had leaked during a pit stop and ignited, setting the front of the car alight and requiring large amounts of extinguisher foam to put it out. Incredibly, no one was hurt and damage to the car was slight. It even rejoined the race, albeit a little scorched, half-an-hour later. Soon after that, Hezemans crashed the

The winning Martini Porsche 935-78 of Jacky Ickx and Jochen Mass runs side-by-side into Woodcote with one of the Gelo-entered Porsche 935-77As.

Gelo 935 he was sharing with Fitzpatrick out of the race. At least they both still had their other car, also driven by Heyer, to concentrate on.

So, at the three-hour mark, Mass and Ickx led from Peterson and Stuck, with Wollek and Pescarolo now third, Ludwig and Bell in fourth, and the Hezemans/Heyer/Fitzpatrick car in fifth. Another BMW 320i, driven by Harald Grohs and Eddy Joosen, was in sixth.

Not long afterwards, we lost the Hezemans/Heyer/Fitzpatrick car when a problem with a wheel hub caused it to pit.

At four hours, guess who was still in the lead?

The Martini 935-78 just kept on going, and had clocked up 156 laps. Behind it, on 152 laps, was the Kremer 935 of Wollek and Pescarolo, with Hezemans, Heyer and Fitzpatrick a lap behind them. In fourth, by virtue of having just made a pit stop, was the Peterson/Stuck BMW. Soon after this, sadly, the car retired – gearless – just as we were looking forward to seeing it fight for second place to the finish.

The contest for the runner-up spot was still alive, though, with Fitzpatrick catching and passing Pescarolo, before retiring in a cloud of smoke soon after. This left another BMW 320 – driven by Freddy Kottulinsky and

Endurance racing at Silverstone in the 1970s & 1980s

The Gelo Porsche 935-77A of Toine Hezemans, Hans Heyer, and John Fitzpatrick ran as high as second, but retired when an oil seal failed.

Markus Hotz – not only in third overall, but also leading the up to 2-litre class. Behind, the Grohs/Joosen BMW was closing, but just failed to catch them, eventually taking a well-deserved fourth overall and second in class.

The Mass/Ickx steamroller just kept on going and took the flag after six hours of racing, while Pescarolo came home second in the Kremer 935, Bob Wollek having switched to the seventh placed Kremer car being driven by Dieter Schornstein and 'John Winter.' See what I meant about confusing for the spectators – knowing who was in which car?

Despite the wealth of Porsche 935s, it was the up to 2-litre BMW 320s that took third and fourth overall. Wollek's switch to the Schornstein/Winter car helped them move up to fifth, while sixth place went to the Franz Konrad and Volkert Merl Porsche 935-77A.

Not a cliff-hanger of a race, but memorable for seeing such a faultless drive from two of the best long-distance sports car drivers of the era, in a glorious looking and sounding machine that was streets ahead of its rivals.

1978

Third overall and victory in the up to 2-litre class went to Harald Grohs and Eddy Joosen in their BMW 320i.

The Kremer-entered Porsche 935-77A of Henri Pescarolo and Bob Wollek took a deserved second place.

23

1979

The following year, the works Porsche team again sent a single-car entry to Silverstone and, once again, it was a glorious machine.

The race this year was opened up to Group 6 sports prototypes as well as the production-based Group 5 cars, although they weren't eligible for points in the World Manufacturers Championship, of which this was the fourth round. Nevertheless, it allowed Porsche to send along a 936 model for Brian Redman and Jochen Mass to drive – the first time we had seen one compete in the UK.

It was expected that, like its 935-78 cousin, the 936 in the colours of Essex Petroleum would probably walk the race. And so it did, for most of the event anyway. It wasn't until almost the final hour that I heard something over the PA about the leader having gone off at Woodcote. I was in a cafe in the paddock having a cup of tea at the time. Typical. I'd stood opposite that spot for hours taking photos and as soon as I leave the biggest incident of the race occurs there. Heigh-ho.

But I'm jumping ahead of myself. Porsche had only decided to contest Le Mans in 1979 at the last minute, and so an entry for the traditional shake-down race – the Silverstone 6-Hours – was essential. The car entered was the very chassis which had emerged victorious in Martini colours at the Le Mans 24-Hours, in both 1976 and '77; the common factor on both occasions being Jacky Ickx. The Belgian was absent from Silverstone, though, the car being placed in the capable hands of Jochen Mass – who had won here for the past two years – and Brian Redman.

The Porsche was on pole by a massive five-and-

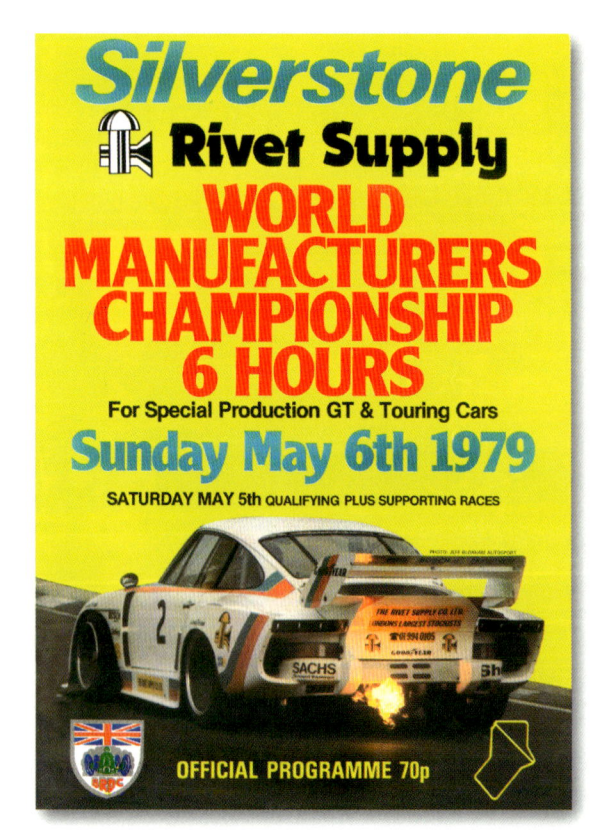

1979 race programme.
(Reproduced with permission from the BRDC)

half-seconds, so we were all expecting a repeat of the previous year's domination by 'Moby Dick' 935. Alongside the 936, on the front row, was the Gelo Porsche 935 of John Fitzpatrick, Bob Wollek and Hans Heyer, while behind them was something a bit different. Opening up the race to Group 6 as well as Group 5 cars added some welcomed variety for British spectators,

1979

The rather heavy Link Aston Martin AMV8 of Derek Bell, David Preece and Robin Hamilton made it to the end, finishing 13th overall.

who had been used to grids full of Porsche 935s at the last few Silverstone races. The Dome Zero RL was a Japanese-entered, Cosworth-powered Group 6 car driven by Gordon Spice and Chris Craft. Alongside them, on the second row, was another Cosworth-powered Group 6 car – the de Cadenet Le Mans of Alain de Cadenet and François Migault.

Manfred Schurti and Bob Wollek shared the second Gelo Porsche 935, which qualified fifth, while in sixth place was the Sekurit team's Porsche 935 driven by Dieter Schornstein and Edgar Doren.

Robin Smith in the Group 6 Chevron Ford B36 he shared with Richard Jones and Laurence Jacobsen. The car retired with engine problems.

25

Endurance racing at Silverstone in the 1970s & 1980s

Seventh on the grid was another newcomer – the Lancia Beta Monte Carlo of Grand Prix driver Riccardo Patrese and rally ace Walter Rohrl – alongside the Chevron B36 of Richard Jones, Robin Smith and Laurence Jacobsen.

There was more variety behind them, with a BMW 320, an Aston Martin V8, and a Lotus Esprit, before the usual ranks of Porsche Carreras and 934s appeared. The grid was smaller than previous years, with only 24 starters, there being 12 non-starters from the original entry list.

It was Fitzpatrick in the Gelo 935 who initially grabbed the lead at the rolling start, but before the lap

Resplendent in its British Racing Green colours, the de Cadenet Le Mans of Alain de Cadenet and François Migault finished in runner-up spot.

John Fitzpatrick at the wheel of the winning Gelo Porsche 935, which he shared with Bob Wollek and Hans Heyer.

was over Mass had demoted him to second. Behind them came Schurti's 935, de Cadenet, Craft in the Dome, Doren's 935 and Smith's Chevron.

The first retirement was the Lancia, with a blown head gasket after just four laps, while a few laps later, de Cadenet moved up to second. By lap 26, Brian Redman in the leading 936 had lapped the entire field. After an hour of racing, his team-mate, Mass, continued to lead. De Cadenet was in second, ahead of the Schurti/Wollek Porsche, followed by the Fitzpatrick/Heyer Porsche, the BMW 320 of Preban Kristofferson and Jens Winther, and the Doren/Schornstein Porsche. The Dome, which looked so promising, had dropped down the field with tyre problems, but was on the move again.

During the second hour, the de Cadenet lost its second place due to an engine misfire, but this was quickly fixed. Meanwhile, the Dome was recovering well and up to fifth place by the two-hour mark. A bit later, the second-placed 935 of Schurti, Wollek and Fitzpatrick suffered a broken turbocharger shaft, and lost nearly three-quarters-of-an-hour in the pits while it was being fixed.

At the halfway point Redman and Mass led by seven laps from de Cadenet and Migault, with Fitzpatrick/Wollek/Heyer in third, another two laps down. In fourth was the Doren/Schornstein 935, ahead of Craft and Spice in the Dome, with Kristofferson and Winther's BMW in sixth.

27

The all-new Dome Zero RL – driven by Chris Craft and Gordon Spice – qualified third and eventually finished in 12th place.

The entry list for the 6-Hour races certainly produced plenty of variety. This is the Lotus Elan of Max Payne and John Evans; it retired with gearbox problems after 96 laps.

1979

Porsches of one sort or another tended to make up the bulk of the entry in these races. This is the Sekurit 935 of Dieter Schornstein and Edgar Doren, which finished third.

Preban Kristoffersen pushes his BMW 320 onto the Woodcote apron after losing oil pressure. The car, co-driven by Jens Winther, was headed for a top six finish prior to this.

Soon after this, we effectively lost two of the most interesting cars in the race. First of all, the Dome was in the pits for almost an hour while it had the gearbox repaired, then the de Cadenet was delayed for ten minutes with brake problems. This allowed the Gelo car up into second. It closed to within a lap of the leading 936 when Redman lost nearly a quarter-of-an-hour in the pits – for bodywork repairs and new rear brake pads – after suffering brake failure going into Stowe Corner and spinning into the catch-fencing. The car rejoined with Mass back behind the wheel.

As we moved into the fifth hour I was standing down at the Woodcote chicane, when the fourth-placed BMW, with Kristofferson at the wheel, coasted to a halt; the Dane got out and pushed the car down the pit lane to retire with engine damage.

29

Brian Redman at the wheel of the works Essex Porsche 936. The car led the race easily (by four laps) until ...

... with just an hour to go, co-driver Jochen Mass crashed heavily at Woodcote. A sorry sight; the wreckage of the historic Porsche 936 chassis, which had won Le Mans in 1976 and '77.

With just over an hour left to run, I went to get a cup of tea and get ready for the finish. It was at this point that Mass crashed heavily right opposite the place where I'd been standing, totally destroying his historic chassis. He had spun violently and without obvious reason as he approached the braking area for Woodcote, slamming heavily into the barrier on the outside of the corner and skating down it before coming to a rest. Once I realised that something had happened, I hurried back to where I'd been standing, on the inside of the corner. There, opposite me, lay a crumpled mess.

That incident left Wollek in the lead from de Cadenet, and that's how it stayed to the end. Schornstein and Doren completed the podium in their 935. The demise of the 936 may have provided a bit of excitement in the last hour, but I was left feeling rather empty and disappointed that a worthy winner of the race had met such an inglorious end.

Bob Wollek brings the winning George Loos-entered Porsche 935, co-driven by John Fitzpatrick and Hans Heyer, into parc fermé at the end of the race.

1980

This was the fifth round of the 1980 World Championship for Makes, and also the fifth round of the World Endurance Challenge for Drivers, the two not always running concurrently during the season. The entry included both Group 5 (production-based) and Group 6 (sports prototype) cars, each class divided at the 2-litre mark, though only Group 5 cars were eligible for the World Championship for Makes.

There was plenty of variety on the grid, especially at the sharp end. On pole position was the Kremer Porsche 935 K3/80, reportedly the fastest example of the car ever built, driven by John Fitzpatrick, Guy Edwards and Axel Plankenhorn. Alongside it was one of the most unusual and attractive designs to contest these endurance races for some time: the Swiss-entered ACR Longines 80 driven by Andre Chevalley, Patrick Gaillard and François Trisconi. Considering the car was untested prior to the race, second on the grid was a good showing.

Behind these two sat a pair of Lancia Beta Monte Carlo Turbos driven by Eddie Cheever/Michele Alboreto and Riccardo Patrese/Walter Rohrl, while next up was a BMW-powered Osella PA8 with Vittorio Brambilla and Lella Lombardi behind the wheel. In sixth place was the Alain de Cadenet/Desire Wilson Cosworth-powered de Cadenet LM.

Edwards in the Kremer 935 K3/80 led away at the start, but it was de Cadenet who shot forward from the third row to snatch second place.

The ACR was unable to capitalise on its front row position, as it suffered ignition problems and pulled off the track at Chapel Curve after just ten minutes. Half-an-hour later, Gaillard had managed to get the car

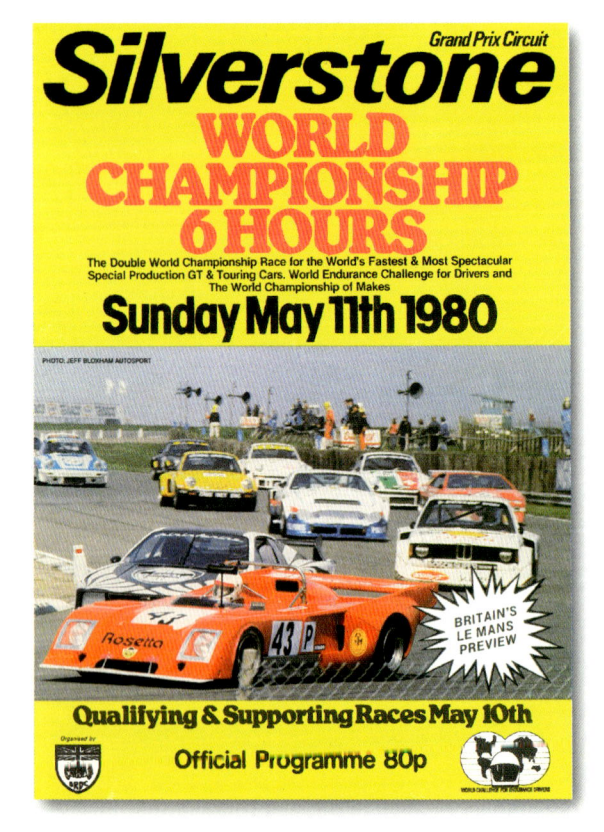

1980 race programme.
(Reproduced with permission from the BRDC)

going and crawled back to the pits. After a change of ignition box, he rejoined to set the fastest lap before being forced to retire at the two-hour mark with clutch problems.

It wasn't the only one in early difficulties either. The two Lancia Beta Monte Carlos both suffered engine misfires, and had to pit after just ten minutes to change

The rear of the field lines up on the grid in sunshine, ready for the midday start.

plugs. After just 45 minutes of racing, Patrese's car lost a wheel at Stowe, causing it to crash heavily – the wheel continued all the way down the track to Club Corner.

At the front, meanwhile, Edwards had pulled out a large lead before handing over to Fitzpatrick, who continued to do the same. This looked like being a bit of a walkover, until the halfway point when the car began to smoke. The de Cadenet, which had been maintaining a strong second place, even taking the lead during the Kremer car's first pit stop, now took over at the head of the field with Desire Wilson at the wheel. After three-and-a-quarter-hours of racing the 935 K3 was finally retired with a damaged piston. This allowed the elderly Porsche 908/3 of Jurgen Barth and Siegfried Brunn to move into second place.

Things weren't going entirely smoothly for the lead de Cadenet though, with a fuel pump problem causing an intermittent misfire, and when Wilson missed the

33

Alain de Cadenet and Desire Wilson took their de Cadenet Le Mans to victory after a close battle with the second-placed Porsche 908/3.

Lella Lombardi and Vittorio Brambilla were out of luck, retiring their Osella-BMW PA8 with ignition problems with just an hour to run.

More variety in the entry. This is the Group 4 Morgan Plus 8 of Richard Down, Bill Stapleton and Bill Wykeham, which, unfortunately, failed to make it to the end.

Jurgen Barth and Siegfried Brunn took their ageing Porsche 908/3 to second overall.

The Group 6 Lola T297 of Nick Faure, Nick Mason, and Peter Clark dives down the inside of the Jacques Guerin/Frederic Alliot/Christian Bussi Porsche 934 at the Woodcote chicane. The Lola failed to finish, while the Porsche came in tenth.

chicane after 183 laps and was given a one lap penalty, suddenly, Barth and Brunn were in the lead. But they, too, were suffering problems in the form of a throttle that wouldn't fully open, and were losing time. Wilson closed in to unlap herself, and when Brunn stopped for a final fuel top-up he got caught behind a slower car, without the power to pass it. Wilson closed inexorably in, egged on by an expectant and excited crowd. With just 23 minutes to go, the de Cadenet outbraked the Porsche into the Woodcote chicane to re-take the lead of the race. Job done, and that was how it stayed to the end, Wilson crossing the line nine seconds ahead of the Porsche.

In third place was the John Paul/Brian Redman Porsche 935 K3, which had been delayed by a tyre problem and an overheating engine. The car eventually crawled over the line, only just making it, while Michele Alboreto and Walter Rohrl brought their sole-surviving Lancia home in fourth.

The crowd revelled in a British victory.

Patrick Neve brings the March BMW M1 he shared with Michael Korten down the pit entrance road. The car retired after a rear puncture damaged the suspension.

Pit stop for the Mike Wilds, Barrie Williams and Adrian Yates-Smith Porsche 911SC. The car eventually retired with engine problems.

The beautiful ACR Longines 80 exits the pits with Patrick Gaillard at the wheel. The car, co-driven by Andre Chevalley and François Trisconi, proved fast but unreliable.

Dieter Schornstein and Harald Grohs took this Vegla Racing Porsche 935 to fifth overall.

1981

I remember the 1981 race specifically for two reasons. Firstly, it teemed down with rain and, secondly, I missed the start because the guy I was travelling up with decided he wanted to stop for a coffee on the way. When we arrived there was a long queue to get into the circuit. "Never mind," he said. "Nothing ever happens at the start of these long races anyway." I left him queuing for the car park and walked in. I arrived breathless at the inside of Woodcote, my favoured position, to see the race favourite, the Jochen Mass Porsche 908/80, buried in the catch-fencing opposite me. He had lost it at the end of the first lap. Race over.

When my friend finally appeared, I motioned towards the wreck on the opposite side of the track. "I thought you said nothing ever happens at the start," I said, bemoaning the fact that, had we arrived on time, I would have been superbly positioned to catch the accident as it happened. Such is life.

Mass, who was sharing the pole-sitting Porsche 908/80 with Reinhold Joest and Volkert Merl, had led away at the start on the streaming wet track, only to lose control under braking at the end of the lap. This meant that, by the time I arrived, it was Guy Edwards in the Lola-Ford T600 – who had been alongside Mass on the front row of the grid – who led the race. Next up, Bobby Rahal, Bob Akin and Peter Lovett in an American-entered Porsche 935, the Lancia Montecarlo of Eddie Cheever and Riccardo Patrese, Tiff Needell, Tony Trimmer and Vivian Candy in an Ibec, Giorgio Francia and Lella Lombardi in an Osella, and Hans Stuck and Hans Heyer in a BMW M1. In other words, a wonderful variety of machinery at the head of the field.

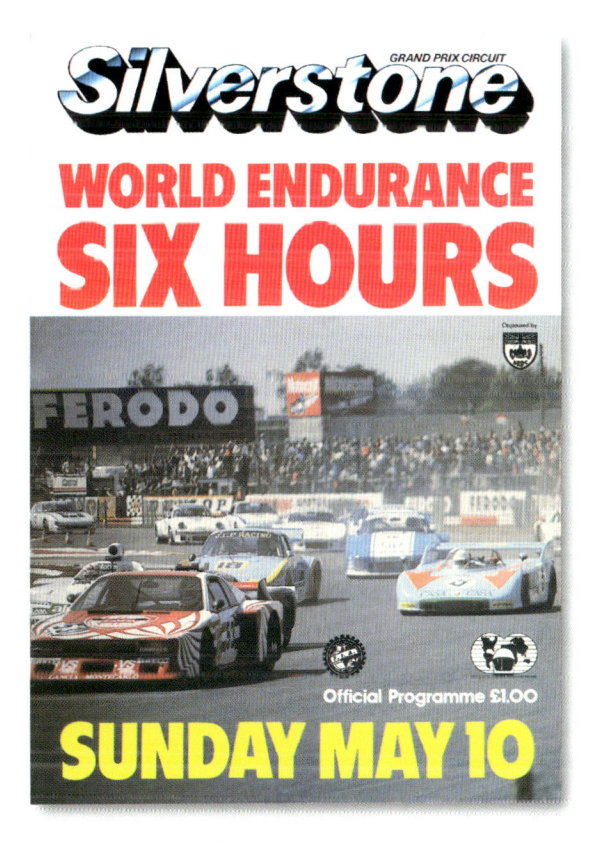

1981 race programme.
(Reproduced with permission from the BRDC)

The treacherous conditions caught out quite a few drivers and caused electrical problems for others, but at the front Edwards continued to pull away. Stuck moved the BMW up into second, ahead of the Porsche 935 of Harald Grohs, Walter Rohrl and Dieter Schornstein which had been making steady progress through the field.

39

Endurance racing at Silverstone in the 1970s & 1980s

After nearly an hour-and-a-half, Stuck took the lead as the Lola pitted. A swift stop for the BMW shortly afterwards allowed Heyer, who had taken over at the wheel, to remain ahead. With the rain coming down harder, though, Emilio de Villota, now driving the Lola, retook first place. The John Cooper/Dudley Wood Porsche 935 moved up into third place, after starting the event in 15th. This was turning into a cracking race!

After two-and-a-half-hours the rain subsided, the track (along with us sodden spectators) was beginning to dry, and some cars began to change onto slick tyres. Soon afterwards, the lead Lola, with de Villota at the wheel, spluttered to a halt out at Abbey with a fuel pick-up problem.

Jens Winther and Lars Viggo Larsen finished 12th overall in this BMW 320.

Rain glints off the soaking wet track as Edgar Doren takes the Porsche 935 through Woodcote, before taking fifth overall with team-mate Jurgen Lassig.

1981

Despite dropping down the field early on, the little Porsche 908/3 of Siegfried Brunn and Eddie Jordan managed to finish third.

It's always a shame when a car that is proving so dominant has to retire, and you feel that whoever subsequently wins the race has inherited the victory, rather than deserving it.

The Lola's demise left the Grohs/Rohrl/Schornstein 935 in the lead, ahead of the Stuck/Heyer BMW. Suddenly, what had looked like an interesting race with a different winner became yet another benefit for the ubiquitous 935.

During the fourth hour the second-placed BMW retired with gear

This is a puzzle. According to all the results and reports of the race, this Belga-sponsored de Cadenet of Alain de Cadenet, Jean-Michel Martin, and Philippe Martin didn't even make it to the grid, retiring with ignition failure. Yet, I managed to get this photo of it, despite having arrived after the start of the race!

41

The Lola-Ford T600 of Guy Edwards and Emilio de Villota led for almost half the race before retiring on the far side of the circuit with a fuel pick-up problem.

The sad sight of the Joest-entered Porsche 908/80 of Jochen Mass, Reinhold Joest, and Volkert Merl which crashed at the end of the first lap.

Lella Lombardi and Giorgio Francia took their Group 6 Osella-BMW PA9 to fourth place.

Win Percy at the wheel of the IMSA GTO class-winning Mazda 253i, which he shared with Yojiro Terada. The car came in eighth overall.

A surprise runner-up was the EMKA BMW M1 of Derek Bell, Steve O'Rourke, and David Hobbs, which also won the IMSA GTX class.

Endurance racing at Silverstone in the 1970s & 1980s

The winning Porsche 935 of Dieter Schornstein, Harald Grohs, and Walter Rohrl looks rather battle-scarred on its way to the chequered flag.

selector trouble, handing the position to Win Percy and Yojiro Terada, who had, amazingly, brought their rotary-powered Mazda 253i through the field. It all went wrong as we approached the five-hour mark, though, when the Mazda and lead Porsche touched and spun at the Woodcote chicane, the Mazda suffering suspension damage.

This meant we had another BMW, in the shape of the Derek Bell/Steve O'Rourke/David Hobbs car, up into second place, with the Cheever/Patrese Lancia in third and closing in. It wasn't to last. At the Lancia's next pit stop a wheel wasn't secured properly and it parted company with the car shortly afterwards.

With just an hour to go the lead 935 was three laps ahead of the second-placed BMW M1, while the little Osella of Lombardi/Francia held third. The Osella was being caught, though, by the elderly Porsche 908/3 of Siegfried Brunn and Eddie Jordan (yes, *the* Eddie Jordan), and with Brunn at the wheel it moved into the final podium place.

That was how it stayed until the end, the German Vegla team 935 taking the last victory for a Group 5 car before the category was phased out at the end of the year. But what a race. Who ever said that endurance racing was dull?

1982

The following year I made sure I was at the track in plenty of time, early enough in fact to make the pre-race pit road walkabout held for holders of paddock transfers between 09.00 and 10.30.

This was the first year of the new Group C category which allowed for purpose-built racing cars with production-based power units. The field still contained entries from Groups 4, 5, and 6, as well as the American IMSA GTX and GTO categories, but only Group C cars could score points for the World Championship for Manufacturers.

It was the best entry ever seen for the event but, as *Autosport* reported in its editorial the following week, the race was a farce.

The reason for this was the fuel-economy regulations introduced for the new category. They stated that teams were only allowed to make five fuel stops in a six-hour race – the same number as in a 1000km event – and the maximum amount of fuel allowed at each stop was 100 litres. The cars were expected to cover over 1100km during the race, so making the fuel last the distance was going to be difficult.

The new 956 from Porsche just looked fantastic. Powered by a 2.6-litre flat-six, twin-turbo engine, it was the first 'ground effect' racing car to be produced by the German company, and it looked resplendent in its Rothmans livery. Jacky Ickx and Derek Bell had managed to snatch pole in the new car from the two Group 6 Lancia Martinis of Piercarlo Ghinzani/Teo Fabi and Michele Alboreto/Riccardo Patrese. In fourth on the grid was another new Group C car, the Ford C100, driven by Manfred Winkelhock and Klaus Ludwig. Behind that was

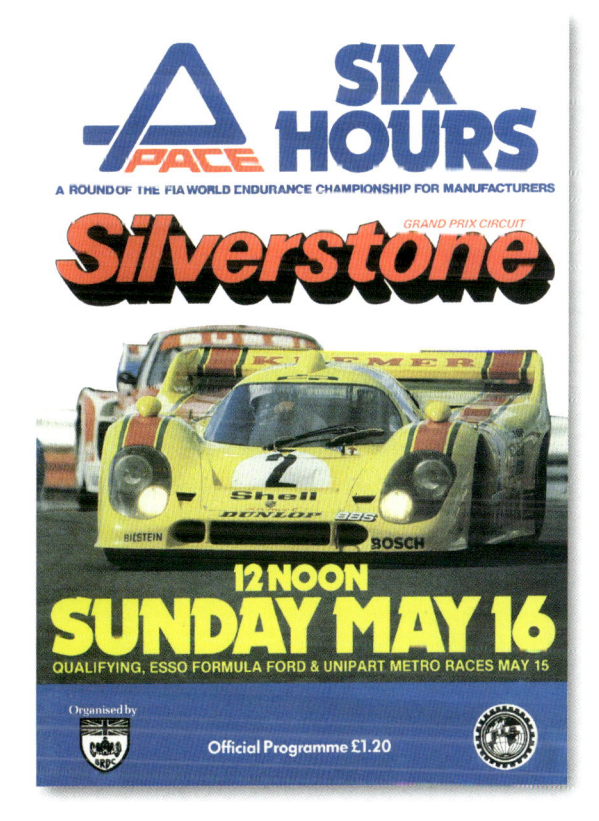

1982 race programme.
(Reproduced with permission from the BRDC)

a Group 6 Osella-BMW PA9/82 (Martino Finotto/Carlo Facetti), then a host of Group C cars, including: a Sauber SHS C6 (Hans Stuck/Hans Heyer); a Porsche 936C (Bob Wollek/Jean-Michel Martin/Philippe Martin), which had been converted to Group C spec; a Lola T610C (Guy Edwards/Rupert Keegan); a Rondeau M382C (Henri Pescarolo/Gordon Spice); and a Grid Plaza S-1

(Emilio de Vilotta/David Hobbs) which completed the top ten.

The Lancia of Ghinzani beat Ickx to the first corner, and his team-mate, Alboreto, got by soon after. However, it was a disastrous start for the two Saubers, with one stuck on the line and the other spinning into the catch-fencing and damaging its rear wing on the first lap.

Behind the two flying Lancias Ickx drove cautiously, conserving fuel until he was back on target and able to push harder once more. Edwards moved up to third in the Lola, before being passed by Winklehock in the Ford.

The lead Lancia had a fright on lap 35 when it almost tripped over a backmarker at the Woodcote chicane and was tipped into a spin.

Because of the need to conserve fuel, none of the cars made a stop until the first hour. The two Lancias still led, ahead of the Pescarolo/Spice Rondeau, and the Winklehock/Ludwig Ford, with

The Belga Joest Porsche 936C of Jean-Michel Martin, Philippe Martin, and Bob Wollek, which eventually finished third, attracted a lot of interest.

The pit road walkabout gave spectators the opportunity to see the cars close up. This is the Porsche 935-78-81 of Gianpiero Moretti and Mauro Baldi, which finished seventh overall and won the IMSA GTX class.

46

The pole-sitting Rothmans Porsche 956 of Jacky Ickx and the Lancia Martini of Piercarlo Ghinzani lead the field round at the end of the pace lap.

Ickx/Bell down in seventh having made their stop. It was dreadful having to watch this magnificent car drone round trying to conserve fuel when we knew that it was capable of fighting for the lead.

Once the first round of pit stops had panned out it was the Lancias still at the head of the field, until Patrese collided with a slower car and suffered a puncture. This caused him to pit and drop behind his team-mate. Alboreto took the wheel and soon put the Lancia back in the lead, until he slowed with battery problems, allowing Ghinzani back in front.

Meanwhile, the Ford C100, which at one point had been up to third place, lost time with a holed radiator.

Halfway through, the Ghinzani/Fabi Lancia was ahead of Patrese/Alboreto, with Ickx/Bell now up into third place. Just after the four hour mark, however, the second-placed Lancia ran into electrical trouble and crawled into the pits. It rejoined, but spluttered to a halt out on the track after a couple of laps and retired. This elevated the carefully driven Porsche of Ickx and Bell into second, with the Pescarolo/Spice Rondeau up to third.

During the final hour, Patrese in the remaining Lancia began to experience clutch problems, and had to nurse his car home, three laps ahead of Ickx in the 956 Porsche. Third eventually went to the Porsche 936C of Martin/Martin/Wollek after the Pescarolo/Spice Rondeau fell back with a broken suspension.

So a farce? A bit harsh, but it certainly wasn't a race.

47

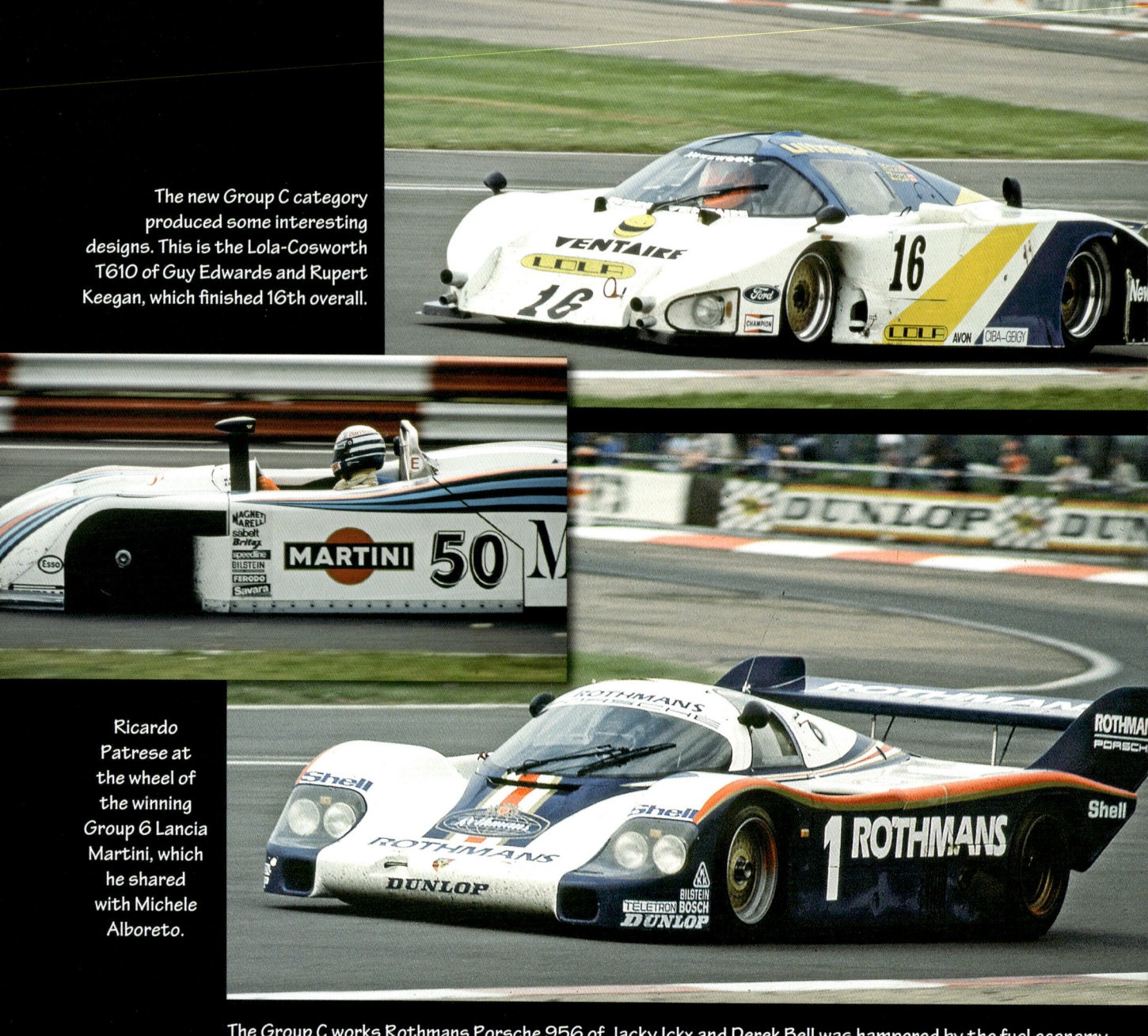

The new Group C category produced some interesting designs. This is the Lola-Cosworth T610 of Guy Edwards and Rupert Keegan, which finished 16th overall.

Ricardo Patrese at the wheel of the winning Group 6 Lancia Martini, which he shared with Michele Alboreto.

The Group C works Rothmans Porsche 956 of Jacky Ickx and Derek Bell was hampered by the fuel economy regulations, and could only finish second.

Ray Mallock and Mike Salmon took their Nimrod Aston Martin to sixth place.

Another new car was the Ford C100 of Klaus Ludwig and Manfred Winklehock, which finished eighth despite a number of delays.

The second-placed Rothmans Porsche 956 of Jacky Ickx and Derek Bell joins the other cars in parc fermé at the end of the race.

1983

This year the regulations changed slightly again, with the race open to Group C, the newly-introduced Group C Junior, and Group B cars. It was the second round of the World Endurance Championship for Manufacturers and Drivers, and also the second round of the European Endurance Championship for Drivers. In addition, and for the first time, it ran as a 1000km distance event as opposed to a six-hour race.

The entry was wonderful. Porsche was not only running a two-car works team, but had made its 956 model available to privateer teams, so we had no fewer than nine examples on the grid. Lancia had produced a Group C car with its LC2 model, and there was a smattering of other machinery, such as a Kremer Porsche C-K5, a Nimrod Aston Martin, and a couple of rotary-engined Mazdas in the Group C Junior class.

It had been raining before the start, leaving the track awash and the teams scratching their heads over the choice of tyres.

Pole had been taken with an incredible lap by the young German driver Stefan Bellof, who was making his debut in the works Rothmans Porsche 956 partnering Derek Bell. Alongside them, but almost two seconds slower, was the Marlboro-liveried 956 of Stefan Johansson and Bob Wollek, with the second works Porsche of Jacky Ickx and Jochen Mass in third. Next up, the two Lancias driven by Michele Alboreto/Riccardo Patrese and Piercarlo Ghinzani/Teo Fabi, followed by a further six Porsche 956s.

The field looked glorious as the cars streamed down in clouds of spray towards Woodcote for the start. By the time they arrived back at the end of the first lap, the two Lancias were a full five seconds ahead of the rest, having

1983 race programme.
(Reproduced with permission from the BRDC)

driven round the front row starters at the first corner, with Alboreto ahead of Ghinzani. The two Rothmans Porsches of Mass and Bell were next up, followed by Wollek and John Fitzpatrick in yet another 956. Halfway round the second lap Ghinzani stole the lead from his team-mate, and a few laps after that Fitzpatrick headed for the pits with a misfire.

Derek Bell in the Rothmans Porsche 956 and Stefan Johansson in the Marlboro-backed car lead the field through the gloom at Woodcote, towards the traditional rolling start.

The two Martini Lancia LC2s of Michele Alboreto and Piercarlo Ghinzani had opened up a tremendous lead by the end of the first lap.

Endurance racing at Silverstone in the 1970s & 1980s

The two Lancias continued to pull away from the rest of the field, but Alan Jones, in the Grand Prix International 956, was on the move. His Dunlop wets were proving ideally suited to the conditions as he moved up to third and began to close on the two Lancias. Ghinzani pitted for slicks on lap 11, but Alboreto stayed out for longer. When he did pit, Jones assumed the lead ahead of the two works Porsches. He stayed in front until lap 19 when Mass went past on the drying track, followed by Bell. We now had the works 956s running 1-2.

These two finally came in on laps 37 and 38, Mass handing over to Ickx and Bell to Bellof. When the first fuel stops were over, Ickx and Bellof led from the 956s of Johansson and Vern Schuppan.

The two Lancias started to run into trouble. Fabi headed for the pits with an overheating engine and Patrese joined him with the same problem. Both cars were worked on for nearly an hour and eventually rejoined before retiring for good, soon after.

This left the works Porsches in front, and Johansson in third. It stayed that way throughout the middle part of the race, until lap 110 when rain began to fall on the far side of the circuit. This caught out Mass, who crashed into the catch-fencing at Club Corner.

The little Group C Junior Mazda 717C of Yojiro Terada and Peter Lovett retired with a broken hub after an hour.

Only two cars were left fighting for the lead, and at the flag it was Bell and Bellof who triumphed, just 35 seconds ahead of the Wollek/Johansson 956 after five hours of racing. Into third came the Canon-sponsored 956 of Jan Lammers and Thierry Boutsen. The Group C Junior class was won by the Alba-Giannini of Martino Finotto and Carlo Facetti.

Rain during an endurance race can be a pain for the spectators in terms of comfort, but it certainly helps to make an entertaining race.

52

Derek Bell scored his first home victory in an endurance sports car race in the works Rothmans Porsche 956 he shared with Stefan Bellof.

Ray Mallock and Mike Salmon finished seventh in their Nimrod Aston Martin C2.

Former Formula One World Champion Alan Jones put in a storming drive in the Grand Prix International Porsche 956 he shared with Vern Schuppan on his way to fifth place.

The Joest Racing New Man Porsche 956 of Hans Heyer and Volkert Merl retired after 74 laps with ignition failure.

Bob Wollek and Stefan Johansson qualified and finished second in the Sorga Racing Marlboro Porsche 956.

1983

The Porsche 930 of Gunther Steckkonig and Bernd Schiller, which finished 15th, 64 laps behind the winner, sits in parc fermé after the race.

1984

A change in the fuel regulations for 1984 meant that, although cars were still limited to a maximum of 600 litres of fuel, there was no limit to the number of fuel stops they could make. This meant that fuel could now be added if a car had to stop for a change of tyres for example. The other change was that the Group C Junior class had been renamed Group C2, with the main class now being referred to as C1.

Over 20,000 spectators turned out for this race, which boasted a record 46-car entry – the biggest outside of the Le Mans 24-Hours, and it created problems in qualifying.

The field was split into the usual mix of Group C1 and C2, with a smattering of GTP, GTX, and Group B cars with a wide variety of makes represented, including: Porsche, Lancia, Lola, Cougar, Sehcar and Nimrod Aston Martin.

Jacky Ickx complained of heavy traffic preventing him getting pole position in the No. 1 works Rothmans Porsche 956-83 he shared with Jochen Mass. He had to settle for second, alongside the pole-sitting Lancia LC2-84 of Bob Wollek and Riccardo Patrese.

One of the beauties of this era of sports car racing was the multitude of different paint jobs on all the privately-entered Porsches, and these filled the next five places.

On the second row was the other works 956-83 of Stefan Bellof and Derek Bell, with Jonathan Palmer and Jan Lammers in the Canon-liveried Richard Lloyd Racing car alongside them. Next up, was Thierry Boutsen and David Hobbs in a Skoal Bandit 956, along with Klaus Ludwig and Henri Pescarolo in a New Man-sponsored

1984 race programme.
(Reproduced with permission from the BRDC)

Joest version. Behind them were Oscar Larrauri and Massimo Sigala in the Team Gaggia car, and the second works Lancia of Mauro Baldi and Paulo Barilla.

The C2 entry was well-supported too, with the Alba-Giannini 002 of Carlo Facetti and Martino Finotto taking class pole.

It was a sunny but breezy day, and the field looked

1984

magnificent as it completed the warming-up lap for the rolling start. It is one of the highlights of an event of this kind to see the pack come streaming through Woodcote, still attempting to hold grid formation as they accelerate hard towards the line for the start of the race.

It was Patrese in the Lancia who grabbed an early lead at Copse, with Mass just behind him. At the end of the first lap these two headed the field from Bell, Palmer, Ludwig, Boutsen and Baldi. Palmer then passed Bell for third on lap two and began to close on the leaders, passing Mass on lap 17. He assumed the lead when Patrese made his first stop for fuel and for mechanics to investigate a misfire – something that was afflicting both Lancias.

With the first round of stops over, Lammers led from Patrese and Ickx, who eventually overtook the misfiring Lancia for second. A short while later, it retired. The Bell/Bellof Porsche lost time when it had to make a second stop with a loose front wheel, dropping out of the top ten.

At lap 50 Lammers led Ickx by over 30 seconds, with Hobbs and the Skoal Bandit 956 of Guy Edwards

Almo Coppelli, Marco Vanoli and Davide Pavia took their Alba-Giannini 001 to 12th overall, winning the Group C2 class.

next up, and Bellof chasing back up the field. Bellof made it up to third, but then, with Bell back behind the wheel, the car had an oil cooler split. This lost them 20 minutes while it was being replaced.

And then it all went wrong for the Canon car at the head of the field. When Palmer came up to lap the third-placed car of Hobbs, there was contact between the two. This wasn't a problem, initially, but a few laps later Palmer pitted with smoke pouring from an oil line that had come adrift.

57

Right: This is the Primagaz Cougar-Ford CO1B of Alain de Cadenet and Yves Courage, which finished 17th after losing time with a broken exhaust.

Below: Ian Harrower, Raymond Taft, and Tom Dodd-Noble brought their ADA-Ford 01 home in 18th place overall and third in Group C2.

This left Ickx in the lead by over a lap from the Rupert Keegan/Guy Edwards Skoal Bandit car, gear selection problems having accounted for the Boutsen/Hobbs 956. On lap 100, Keegan spun at the chicane, handing second to Pescarolo and Ludwig.

And that's how it stayed to the end, with the Alba-Giannini 001 of Almo Coppelli, Marco Vanoli and Davide Pavia winning Group C2.

1984

You're not meant to take photos from the bridge over the circuit, but I found a hole in the side just large enough for the camera lens. Four Porsche 956s speed out of Woodcote, onto the main straight.

Rupert Keegan spun the Skoal Bandit Porsche 956 he was sharing with Guy Edwards at the chicane, losing second place as a result.

Pit stop for the Group B Porsche 928S of Raymond Boutinaud, Philippe Renault, and Gilles Guinant. The car eventually retired with engine problems.

1985

The renamed World Endurance Championship gathered at Silverstone on 12 May 1985 for what was the third round of the drivers' title chase, but only the second of the teams' championship.

The race had a strong entry for both Group C1 and C2, with no fewer than 13 Porsche 956/962s and a pair of Lancia LC2-85s forming the bulk of the top class. C2 included cars from Spice, Ecosse, Gebhardt, Tiga, Alba and Mazda, among others.

Heading the entry, as usual, was the pair of works Rothmans Porsche 962Cs, with Jacky Ickx and Jochen Mass in the No. 1 car and Derek Bell and Hans Stuck in the sister car. Heading the grid, however, was the pair of works Martini Lancia LC2-85s, with Riccardo Patrese/Alessandro Nannini on pole and Bob Wollek/Mauro Baldi alongside. Third was the Bell/Stuck works Porsche, while the Kremer 962C of Manfred Winkelhock and Marc Surer was in fourth. Behind them sat Jonathan Palmer and Jan Lammers with the Richard Lloyd Racing, Canon-sponsored 956 GTi. Sixth on the grid was Thierry Boutsen and Walter Brun in the Brun 962.

The two Lancias headed the field as they swept out of Woodcote at the traditional rolling start, but Winkelhock slipped his 962 inside Patrese's Lancia at Becketts to steal second place behind Wollek. By the end of the lap though, Patrese was back into second, so it was a Martini-Lancia one-two as they crossed the line for the first time. Winkelhock was third, ahead of Palmer and Boutsen, while the two Rothmans Porsches were down in eighth and tenth.

The man on the move, though, was Palmer in the

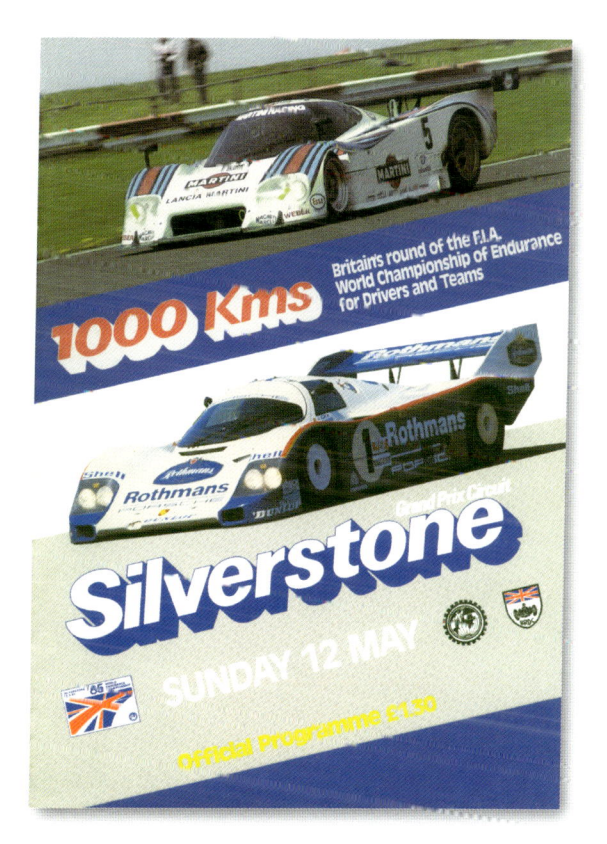

1985 race programme.
(Reproduced with permission from the BRDC)

Canon Porsche, battling his way up to second and engaging in a furious fight with the two Lancias until he emerged in the lead on lap ten. Meanwhile, Wollek in third was under pressure from Boutsen, while Oscar Larrauri in a Brun 956B was disputing fifth place with Winkelhock and Klaus Ludwig in the Joest 956B. This was more like a sprint race than an endurance event,

The Ceekar 83JI of Max Payne and Chris Ashmore sits on the grid just prior to the start. The car suffered fuel pick-up problems during the race, but still finished fifth in Group C2 and 15th overall.

The Richard Lloyd Racing Canon Porsche 956GTi of Jonathan Palmer and Jan Lammers was one of the quickest cars on track, but also one of four 956s to lose a wheel during the race. It eventually finished fifth.

and in sharp contrast to some of the earlier Silverstone races in which one car had dominated.

Boutsen's challenge came to an abrupt end on lap 14 when he lost his left front wheel under braking for Stowe Corner, and limped back to the pits. A lap later, Jo Gartner's ninth-placed Porsche also lost a wheel. Palmer, meanwhile, was pulling away at the front of the field and, despite his pace, was one of the last to pit during the first round of fuel stops – handing over to Jan Lammers. The Dutchman now led from Nannini and Baldi in the Lancias, followed by Ludwig, Surer and Ickx in the first of the Rothmans cars.

The C2 Class was being led by the Bovis Ecosse

Jacky Ickx and Jochen Mass in the No 1 Rothmans 962C led home a Porsche one-two ahead of Derek Bell and Hans Stuck in the sister car.

C2/85 of Mike Wilds and Ray Mallock, ahead of the Spice-Tiga GC85 driven by Ray Bellm and Gordon Spice.

Lammers held the lead until the second round of stops, handing back to Palmer, and now Patrese began to close in. He took the lead on lap 88 when Palmer was slowed by a backmarker, but the Canon car was back in front four laps later. This was gripping stuff. The pair continued to dice until lap 103, when yet another left front wheel went flying through the air – this time belonging to Palmer's leading Porsche. It was particularly galling as exactly the same thing had happened to the pair at the previous round at Monza when they had been leading.

This left Patrese well clear of team-mate Wollek, but now lurking in third and fourth, having had a steady run to conserve fuel, were the two Rothmans Porsches of Ickx and Bell. The latter lost a little time in the pits having the windscreen secured and dropped to fifth.

After the third round of stops Nannini was driving the leading Lancia, with a gap back to team-mate Baldi, and Ickx still in third. Surer was now fourth, being pursued by Stuck, who was keen to make up for lost time.

Things settled down for a while until the second-placed Lancia, now with bodywork damage, came in for an early fuel stop and resumed in fifth. Then on lap 148, disaster struck the leading Lancia of Nannini when it limped into the pits with a seized right front wheel bearing, eventually rejoining in seventh place. The two Rothmans cars had also pitted, meaning that the leader was now Bob Wollek in the second Lancia, with

The Torno Porsche 962C of Thierry Boutsen and Walter Brun was another of the Porsches to shed a wheel, losing nine laps in the pits and eventually finishing tenth.

The Ecosse-Ford C2/85 of Ray Mallock and Mike Wilds won the Group C2 class, finishing ninth overall.

Stanley Dickens shared this Strandell-Porsche with Martin Schanche, the pair finishing a very respectable third in Group C2 and 13th overall.

The Gebhardt-Ford JC843 of Ian Harrower, Steve Earle, and Mark Galvin retired after catching fire when oil leaked onto the hot exhaust.

David Kennedy and Yojiro Terada took their rotary-engined Mazda 737C to 16th place overall.

The Brun Motorsport Porsche 956B of Massimo Sigala and Oscar Larrauri ran well, until a rear tyre failure caused it to crash into the catch-fencing at Stowe.

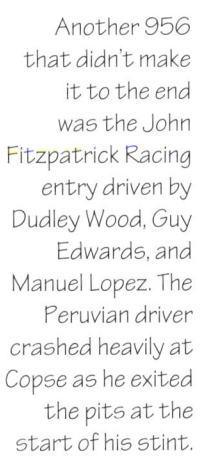

Another 956 that didn't make it to the end was the John Fitzpatrick Racing entry driven by Dudley Wood, Guy Edwards, and Manuel Lopez. The Peruvian driver crashed heavily at Copse as he exited the pits at the start of his stint.

66

The works Rothmans Porsche drivers Hans Stuck and Jacky Ickx stand next to the winning car in parc fermé. The pair finished first and second, albeit a lap apart.

the Oscar Larrauri/Massimo Sigala 956B just behind, until it made its next fuel stop. Mass, who was now second, closed on Wollek and took the lead when the Lancia made its next scheduled stop – Wollek handing over to Baldi. The other Rothmans Porsche of Bell and Stuck moved up to second.

So we had the works 962Cs running first and second, despite having been well down the field in the opening stages. But both still had to make final stops, whereas Baldi's Lancia could run to the finish. Except it didn't. On lap 184 the Porsches pitted, and as Ickx rejoined, Baldi was coming out of the chicane. We were set for an epic chase to the flag between the three leading cars until Baldi slowed along the pit straight, his car jammed in gear due to a broken gearbox oil cooler.

That left Ickx and Mass to lead home Bell and Stuck a lap behind. Third went to the Lancia of Patrese and Nannini, which caught and passed the Winklehock/Surer Porsche with a lap to go. Into fifth came the charging Jonathan Palmer and Jan Lammers, the former breaking the lap record as he stormed through the field after their earlier delays. Sixth place went to the Klaus Ludwig/Paulo Barilla/Paul Belmondo Porsche 956B.

The C2 category was won by Ray Mallock and Mike Wilds in their Ecosse, with Gordon Spice and Ray Bellm second in their Spice-Tiga.

1986

Silverstone on Monday 5 May 1986 was definitely the place to be if you were an endurance racing fan with any sense of history, for it was the day that the Jaguar name returned to the winners' circle for the first time since 1957. On the showery Bank Holiday Monday morning, 26,000 fans turned out hoping for a Jaguar victory on home soil – and weren't disappointed.

The entry was headed by the pair of works Rothmans Porsche 962Cs of Derek Bell/Hans Stuck and Jochen Mass/Bob Wollek, but it was the Martini Lancia LC2-86 of Alessandro Nannini and Andrea de Cesaris which claimed pole position in qualifying. Alongside them was the Bell/Stuck Porsche, while heading the second row – much to the crowd's delight – was the Silk Cut Jaguar XJR-6 of Derek Warwick and Eddie Cheever. Next up, Jo Gartner and Tiff Needell in a Kremer-entered Porsche 962C and the second Jaguar of Jean-Louis Schlesser and Gianfranco Brancatelli. Completing the third row was yet another 962C, this time the Joest-entered car of George Follmer, John Morton and Paulo Barilla.

At the start there seemed to be a lot of bumping and barging as the pack crossed the line, and the Cougar of Pierre-François Rousselot spun at Woodcote on the damp track before it even got that far, but fortunately nobody hit it.

So it was the Lancia of Nannini which led at the end of the first lap from Warwick's Jaguar, Gartner's Porsche, the 962C of Bell, and the second Jaguar of Schlesser, who was soon past the Rothmans car and up to fourth. The instant acceleration of the normally-aspirated Jaguars seemed to more than make up for their lack

1986 race programme.
(Reproduced with permission from the BRDC)

of turbo power, while the Lancias and Porsches had to contend with 'turbo lag' and wait for the power to come in. On lap six Schlesser also passed Gartner, and closed in on his team-mate. This was looking good.

Warwick gradually closed in on the leading Lancia – urged on by the crowd – until the first pit stops when he took the lead as Nannini stopped, only to pit himself a lap later. The cars rejoined with de Cesaris in the Lancia and Cheever chasing him down in the Jaguar, just two seconds adrift. Finally, on lap 49 a Jaguar led the race for real – you can imagine the home crowd's reaction. The Schlesser/Brancatelli Jaguar was back in third, these three being the only ones still on the lead lap.

Cheever maintained his lead until he handed back over to Warwick, and Nannini – now back behind the wheel of the Lancia – emerged ahead, albeit only by a couple of seconds. Warwick closed the gap and fought his way past until Nannini retook the lead a few laps later. Bear in

The Primagaz Couger-Porsche C-12 of Pierre-François Rousselot and Yves Courage is wheeled onto the grid.

Spectators and mechanics look on expectantly as the cars move off on the pace lap.

Running just behind the leading bunch, the Rothmans Porsche 962C of Bob Wollek leads Oscar Larrauri's 962C, the Sauber-Mercedes C-8 of Mike Thackwell, and the Porsche 956B of George Follmer through the Woodcote chicane.

mind that this was an endurance race and the pair were scrapping as if it were a sprint, when it was only about half-distance.

Warwick retook the lead again with 100 laps on the board. The second Jaguar, with Schlesser aboard, had been closing on the leading pair but lost time in the pits with gear linkage problems. As Warwick pitted, Nannini took the lead again, until his next scheduled stop where the car was delayed by a change of brake pads. When it returned to the track, with de Cesaris at the wheel, instead of gaining ground on the lead Jaguar, it began to fall further back, until it eventually pitted with fuel pressure problems.

This left Warwick and Cheever comfortably ahead, and that's how it stayed until the flag. Derek Bell and Hans Stuck brought their Rothmans Porsche home second, with Jo Gartner and Tiff Needell third in their Kremer 962C.

But all eyes were on the Jaguars. The Schlesser/Brancatelli car, although down in seventh place after its delays, was circulating in tandem with that of Warwick/Cheever, and the pair crossed the line in a formation finish that brought the crowd to its feet. Jaguar had won a world championship event for the first time in 29 years, and we had been there to witness it.

The GTP class-winning rotary-engined Mazda 757 of Yoshimi Katayama and Yojiro Terada finished in 13th place overall.

The Castrol URD-BMW C-83 of Jens Winther and David Mercer finished fourth in Group C2 and 18th overall.

Group C2 winners were Ray Bellm and Gordon Spice in their Spice-Cosworth SC86C, finishing in 14th place overall.

The ninth-placed Brun Motorsport Porsche 956 of Walter Brun and Frank Jelinski looked glorious in the colours of Jägermeister.

Derek Warwick in the Silk Cut Jaguar XJR-6 takes the lead from the Martini Lancia LC2-86 of Alessandro Nannini going into the Woodcote chicane.

Jurgen Lassig spins the Obermaier Porsche 956 he co-drove with Fulvio Ballabio and Dudley Wood at the chicane. The car eventually finished in 12th place.

Jo Gartner, seen here climbing out of the third-placed Kremer Porsche 962C in parc fermé, was to lose his life at Le Mans a few weeks later.

73

1987

Jaguar returned to the scene of its previous year's success with three victories already under its belt in the 1987 season. The team had a new car, the XJR-8, and it had already beaten the previously all-conquering Porsches at Jarama, Jerez and Monza. Ahead of it, after Silverstone, lay the Le Mans 24-Hours, and the TWR team which ran the cars were determined to go there on a high.

It was a cold and windy day, but 23,000 spectators still turned up. The circuit had been revised since the previous year, with a new slow left-right dog-leg just before Woodcote to slow the cars down. With this new section of track in place, which gave photographers like me the chance to capture the cars close up and going slower, the old chicane was no longer used.

There were three Silk Cut Jaguars on hand, two of the regular XJR-8s for last year's winner, Eddie Cheever, partnered this time by Raul Boesel, and one for Jan Lammers who was driving with John Watson. Plus, there was also a low-drag Le Mans version, the XJR-8LM driven by Martin Brundle and John Nielsen.

The works Porsches were backed by Shell and race sponsor Autoglass this year, and there were two 962Cs for the regular pairings of Derek Bell/Hans Stuck and Jochen Mass/Bob Wollek. The Bell/Stuck car qualified on pole, while alongside it, making its debut, was the Kouros Sauber-Mercedes C9 in the hands of Mike Thackwell and Henri Pescarolo. The Mass/Wollek Porsche was third, followed by the first of the Jaguars – the Cheever/Boesel car; the turbocharged Porsches and Sauber proved faster on the long sweeps of Silverstone than the normally-aspirated Jaguars.

The Group C2 entry was stronger than C1, with 15

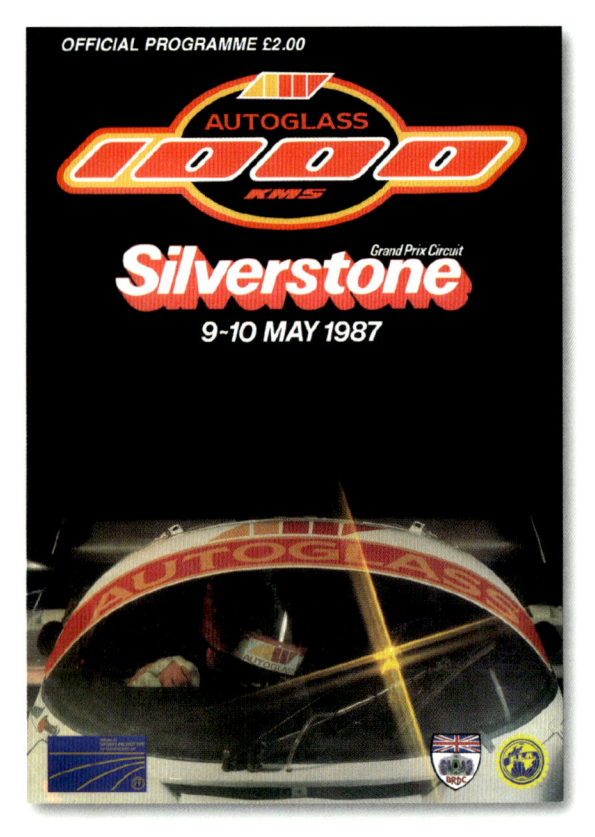

1987 race programme. (Reproduced with permission from the BRDC)

cars to the 11 C1s, and pole went to Gordon Spice and Fermin Velez in their Spice SE86C.

At the start it was Thackwell in the Sauber-Mercedes who led into Copse Corner from Stuck's Porsche, and then the Jaguars of Cheever and Lammers. At the end of the lap Thackwell still led from Stuck, Cheever, Lammers, and Mass. On the second lap both

1987

Cheever and Lammers got past Stuck, but Thackwell proved more difficult – the Sauber slowly pulling away until Cheever began to close the gap a few laps later and get on its tail. He eventually got past on lap 17. While this was going on, Jonathan Palmer in the Liqui Moli Porsche had been on the move. He had got up to fourth before losing power and finally retiring.

At the front, Cheever opened up a gap as Thackwell had to ease off to conserve fuel, eventually being passed by Lammers for second place. After the first round of pit stops the Cheever/Boesel Jaguar led from the Lammers/Watson car, with Pescarolo now driving the Sauber in third. This didn't last, however, as the black car developed a misfire which dropped it back. It eventually retired with rear suspension failure when Thackwell was back behind the wheel.

On lap 50, we had the wonderful sight of the Jaguars running first, second and third. John Nielsen had taken the XJR-8LM past Bell's Porsche 962, although

The Porsche 962 GTi of Mauro Baldi and the Rothmans 962 of Jochen Mass negotiate the new chicane during the untimed morning warm-up.

Jan Lammers in his Silk Cut Jaguar XJR8 leads Mike Thackwell's Kouros Sauber-Mercedes C9 during the warm-up session.

The Swiftair Ecosse team lines up side-by-side on the grid while the national anthem is played.

at the second round of pit stops Hans Stuck regained the place. After 129 laps Boesel came into the pits with a puncture and dropped to third behind the Porsche.

It got a bit confusing towards the end of the race after Nielsen's Jaguar collided with the Brun Motorsport Torno Porsche 962 of Massimo Sigala. Nielsen headed pitwards for a new nose but the 962 was beached in the gravel trap at Copse, bringing out the safety car. Stuck and Watson both pitted, which meant that Boesel was still in the lead with Lammers second – leaving the lead XJR-8 out-of-synch with the others on fuel stops.

The Liqui Moli Porsche 962 GTi of Jonathan Palmer and Mauro Baldi sits in the pits as mechanics try to solve an engine problem. The car was eventually retired, having completed just 25 laps.

Mechanics work on the Primagaz Cougar-Porsche C20 of Herve Regout and Yves Courage in its pit garage. Gearbox problems caused its retirement.

Pit stop for the second-placed Silk Cut Jaguar XJR8 of Jan Lammers and John Watson.

Endurance racing at Silverstone in the 1970s & 1980s

Vito Veninata, Pasquale Barberio and Ranieri Randaccio brought their Group C2 Tiga-Cosworth GC85, seen here being passed by one of the Jaguars, home in tenth place.

When they had finally made all their stops, and swapped the lead a couple of times in the process, it was the Cheever/Boesel car out in front by just six seconds from Lammers and Watson.

We thought that was it, but then, just 15 laps from the end, there was an almighty crash on the main straight involving the Brun Porsche of Oscar Larrauri and the C2 Tiga of Bruno Sotty. The other cars had to weave through the debris for a couple of laps before the pace car was again sent out. This meant that the two leading Jags were nose-to-tail with just 11 laps to run when they were unleashed again, the Stuck/Bell 962 a lap down in third.

Cheever held his team-mate at bay until, with just six laps left, they were given the signal from the Jaguar pit to hold position. That was how it stayed, the pair crossing the line in formation. Ray Mallock and David Leslie took a deserved but narrow victory in the C2 class in their Swiftair Ecosse C286, ahead of the Gordon Spice/Fermin Velez Spice.

1987

Eddie Cheever in the winning Silk Cut Jaguar XJR8 he shared with Raul Boesel.

The two Silk Cut Jaguar XJR8s of Eddie Cheever and Jan Lammers negotiate the new chicane on their way to a resounding one-two victory.

1988

And so, to the last long-distance endurance race to be held at the circuit that decade, though we didn't realise it at the time. Race day was wet and miserable to start with, although it didn't deter around 35,000 of us making the trip to Northamptonshire (or Buckinghamshire if you were watching from the southern end of the circuit since it spans the two counties).

It was the Sauber-Mercedes C9-88 of Jean-Louis Schlesser and Jochen Mass on pole, with the Jaguar XJR-9 of Martin Brundle and Eddie Cheever, who was on for a hat-trick of wins in the event, alongside them. On the second row was Mauro Baldi and James Weaver in the second Sauber, along with the fastest of the Porsches, the Bob Wollek/Philippe Streiff/David Hobbs Blaupunkt Joest 962.

Behind them sat Derek Bell and Tiff Needell in the Richard Lloyd Racing 962GTi and the second of the Jaguars, driven by Jan Lammers and Johnny Dumfries. Then came the Kremer Porsche of Kris Nissen/Harald Grohs and the Joest entry of Frank Jelinski/Stanley Dickens/'John Winter.' Behind them on the fifth row, was the Mazda 767C of David Kennedy/Yojiro Terada/Yoshimi Katayama and the fastest of the C2 class, the Spice Cosworth SE87C of Costos Los/Wayne Taylor.

The rain had stopped before the 1.00pm start, leaving a damp track, but it was still grey and overcast as the Jaguar XJS pace car led the field round on the warm-up lap – all except for the Spice of Costos Los, which refused to fire up and was pushed into the pit lane.

The rolling start of these races never ceased to thrill me, and this was no exception. Schlesser and Cheever

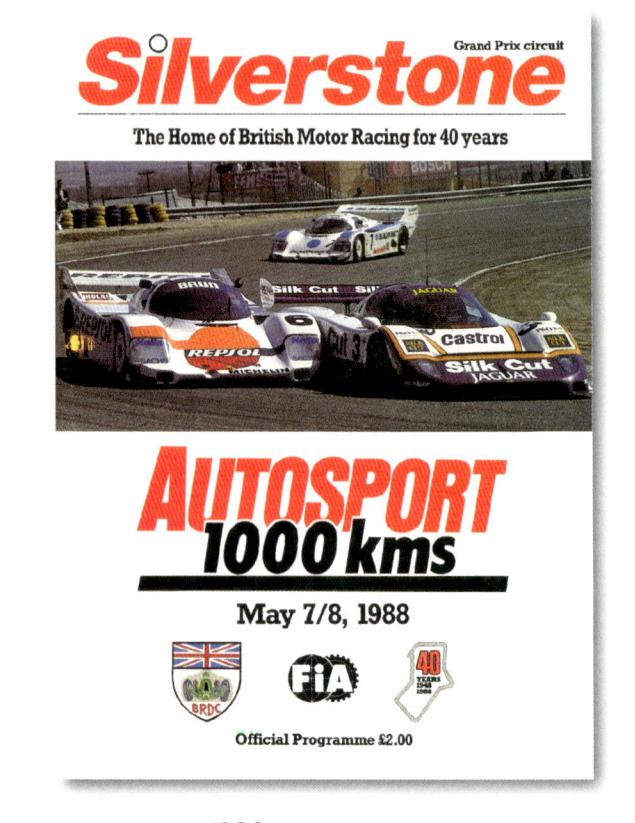

1988 race programme.
(Reproduced with permission from the BRDC)

went into Copse side-by-side, the Sauber just emerging ahead, while Baldi and Wollek fought over third place. At the end of the first lap, it was Sauber-Jaguar-Sauber-Porsche.

The opening laps were quite extraordinary, more akin to a ten-lap Formula Ford sprint than the opening stint of a 1000 kilometre endurance race. Schlesser,

1988

Cheever and Baldi broke away from the rest of the field and the race was all about these three. After seven frantic laps Cheever pushed his way past the Sauber, and Baldi immediately relegated Schlesser to third before taking the lead from Cheever – only to have the American steal it back moments later. Not long after that, Schlesser retook second from Baldi and then assumed the lead from Cheever. Less than half-an-hour had gone by and we had already had three different leaders, and they were still scrapping.

As they came up to lap backmarkers it all changed again, with the Jaguar dropping to third as the two Saubers battled furiously. We all wondered how long it would go on, and whether or not it would end in tears. Behind them, meanwhile, Wollek and Lammers had been battling over fourth, with the Jaguar eventually pulling away leaving Wollek to fight off a challenge from Derek Bell.

The Joest Blaupunkt Porsche 962 of Frank Jelinski, which he co-drove to fifth place with Stanley Dickens and 'John Winter,' enters the pit lane with front end damage early in the race.

Tom Dodd-Noble, in the Group C2 ADA-Cosworth 03 he shared with 'Stingbrace' and Colin Pool, was also in the wars early on. The car finished the race, but was not classified.

81

Philippe Streiff, Bob Wollek and David Hobbs brought their Joest Blaupunkt Porsche 962 home in fourth place.

A hat-trick for Jaguar, taking victory for the third time in as many years. This is Martin Brundle in the winning XJR9 he shared with Eddie Cheever.

David Kennedy, Yojiro Terada and Yoshimi Katayama were victorious in the GTP class in their rotary-engined Mazda 767C, finishing an excellent ninth overall.

The Group C2 winner was the Spice-Cosworth SE88C of Thorkild Thyrring and Almo Coppelli, which finished in sixth place overall.

At the first pit stops Schlesser handed over to Mass, Cheever to Brundle, and Baldi to Weaver, but because of the slick pit work by the Jaguar crew, it was Brundle who emerged in front and began to pull away. By the time he handed back to Cheever he was 30 seconds ahead of Mass, and the race, barring accidents, was effectively won.

In fact, both Jaguars were flying now. Dumfries in the No. 2 car had caught Weaver's Sauber and was challenging for third place. As Dumfries attempted to pass, the cars touched, resulting in body damage to the Jaguar which, nevertheless, took the place. It stayed this way until six laps from the end when Dumfries, who had been trying to catch the second-placed Sauber to make it a Jaguar 1-2, ran out of fuel and had to park out on the circuit.

The gap between first and second remained constant at half-a-minute, and Cheever achieved his hat-trick of wins in the event, ahead of the two Saubers. Bell and Needell came in fourth but were subsequently disqualified for using too much fuel, caused by a faulty delivery meter in their fuelling rig. That handed fourth to the Wollek/Streiff/Hobbs Porsche, ahead of their team-mates Jelinski/Dickens/'Winter.' In sixth was the C2-winning Spice-Cosworth SE88C of Thorkild Thyrring and Almo Coppelli.

The latter half of the race might not have been thrilling, but those opening laps certainly stayed in the memory and, anyway, it had been another Jaguar victory, so what more could we have asked for?

The AEG Olympia Sauber-Mercedes C9-88 drivers, Mauro Baldi and James Weaver, had to settle for third place after a spirited drive.

Derek Bell and Tiff Needell finished fourth on the track in the RLR Porsche 962 GTi-200, but were disqualified in post-race scrutineering for using too much fuel.

Results

1976 World Championship for Manufacturers 6-Hours, Sunday 9 May

Position	Drivers	Car	Laps	Distance	Average speed
1	John Fitzpatrick/Tom Walkinshaw	BMW 3.5 CSL	217.20	636.83 miles	106.14mph
2	Bob Wollek/Hans Heyer	Porsche 935	217.16	–	–
3	Egon Evertz/Leo Kinnunen	Porsche Carrera RSR	215.66	–	–
4	Harald Grohs/Hughes de Fierlandt	BMW 3.5 CSL	213.17	–	–
5	Lella Lombardi/Heinz Martin	Porsche Carrera RSR	205.96	–	–
6	Umberto Grano/Martino Finotto	Ford Escort	199.59	–	–

Fastest lap Jacky Ickx (Martini Porsche 935), 1m28.19s (119.68mph)
Class wins 3001cc-6000cc: Fitzpatrick/Walkinshaw, 106.14mph
  2001cc-3000cc: Kurt Simonsen/Kenneth Leim (Porsche Carrera RSR), 92.09mph
  Up to 2000cc: Grano/Finotto, 97.53mph

1977 Kosset World Manufacturers 6-Hours, Sunday 15 May

Position	Drivers	Car	Laps	Distance	Average speed
1	Jochen Mass/Jacky Ickx	Porsche 935-77	230.01	674.39 miles	112.40mph
2	Bob Wollek/John Fitzpatrick	Porsche 935	220.84	–	–
3	Rolf Stommelen/Toine Hezemans	Porsche 935	222.17	–	–
4	Ronnie Peterson/Helmut Kelleners	BMW 320i	215.67	–	–
5	Franz Konrad/Peter Hahnlein	Porsche 935	214.35	–	–
6	Martino Finotto/Carlo Facetti	Porsche 935	211.31	–	–

Fastest lap Mass, 1m27.28s (120.93mph)
Class wins 3001cc-6000cc: Ickx/Mass, 112.40mph
  2001cc-3000cc: Kenneth Leim/Kurt Simonsen (Porsche Carrera RSR), 100.19mph
  Up to 2000cc: Peterson/Kelleners, 105.39 mph
Group wins Groups 2/4: Vittorio Brambilla/Gianpiero Moretti (Porsche 934), 101.92mph
  Groups 1/3: Tony Wingrove/Peter Lovett (Porsche Carrera), 92.91mph

Endurance racing at Silverstone in the 1970s & 1980s

1978 World Manufacturers 6-Hours, Sunday 14 May

Position	Drivers	Car	Laps	Distance	Average speed
1	Jochen Mass/Jacky Ickx	Porsche 935-78	235	689.49 miles	114.91mph
2	Bob Wollek/Henri Pescarolo	Porsche 935-77A	228	–	–
3	Harald Grohs/Eddy Joosen	BMW 320i	219	–	–
4	Freddy Kottulinsky/Markus Hotz	BMW 320i	219	–	–
5	Dieter Schornstein/'John Winter'/Bob Wollek	Porsche 935-76A	218	–	–
6	Franz Konrad/Volkert Merl	Porsche 935-77A	202	–	–

Fastest lap Mass, 1m23.88s (125.84mph)
Class wins Over 2000cc: Mass/Ickx, 114.91mph
Up to 2000cc: Grohs/Joosen, 107.10mph
Group wins Groups 3/4: Eberhard Sindel/Preben Kristofferson (Porsche 934), 96.53mph
Groups 1/2: Dave Brodie/Dave Matthews (Ford Capri), 89.05mph

1979 Rivet Supply World Manufacturers Championship 6-Hours, Sunday 6 May

Position	Drivers	Car	Laps	Distance	Average speed
1	John Fitzpatrick/Bob Wollek/Hans Heyer	Porsche 935	228	670.453 miles	111.74mph
2	Alain de Cadenet/François Migault	de Cadenet Cosworth	216	–	–
3	Dieter Schornstein/Edgar Doren	Porsche 935	216	–	–
4	Jean-Pierre Delaunay/Cyril Grandet	Porsche Carrera RSR	209	–	–
5	Manfred Schurti/John Fitzpatrick/Bob Wollek	Porsche 935	209	–	–
6	Peter Zbinden/Edi Kofel	Porsche 934	209	–	–

Fastest lap Jochen Mass (Porsche 936), 1m 23.25s (126.79mph)
Class wins Over 2000cc: Fitzpatrick/Wollek/Heyer, 117.74mph
Up to 2000cc: no finishers
Group wins Group 6: de Cadenet/Migault, 108.40mph
Group 5: Fitzpatrick/Wollek/Heyer, 117.74mph
Groups 3/4: Delauney/Grandet, 107.37mph

Results

1980 Silverstone 6-Hours, Sunday 11 May

Position	Drivers	Car	Laps	Distance	Average speed
1	Alain de Cadenet/Desire Wilson	de Cadenet-Cosworth LM	236	*687.61 miles	114.60mph
2	Siegfried Brunn/Jurgen Barth	Porsche 908/3	236	–	–
3	John Paul/Brian Redman	Porsche 935 K3	235	–	–
4	Michele Alboreto/Walter Rohrl	Lancia Beta Monte Carlo	233	–	–
5	Dieter Schornstein/Harald Grohs	Porsche 935	230	–	–
6	Edgar Doren/Jurgen Lassig/Gerhard Holup	Porsche 935	226	–	–

Fastest lap: John Fitzpatrick (Porsche 935 K3/80), 1m25.530s (123.45mph)

Class wins:
- Over 2000cc: de Cadenet/Wilson, 114.60mph
- Up to 2000cc: Alboreto/Rohrl, 113.09mph

Group wins:
- Group 6: de Cadenet/Wilson, 114.60mph
- Group 5: Alboreto/Rohrl, 113.09mph
- Group 4: Richard Cleare/Tony Dron (Porsche 934), 100.61mph
- GTP: no finishers
- IMSA: John Paul Snr/Brian Redman (Porsche 935), 113.95mph

*Including one lap penalty

1981 Silverstone World Endurance 6-Hours, Sunday 10 May

Position	Drivers	Car	Laps	Distance	Average speed
1	Dieter Schornstein/Harald Grohs/Walter Rohrl	Porsche 935	206	602.08 miles	100.35mph
2	Derek Bell/Steve O'Rourke/David Hobbs	BMW M1	204	–	–
3	Siegfried Brunn/Eddie Jordan	Porsche 908/3	204	–	–
4	Lella Lombardi/Giorgio Francia	Osella-BMW PA9	201	–	–
5	Edgar Doren/Jurgen Lassig	Porsche 935	200	–	–
6	Bob Akin/Bobby Rahal/Peter Lovett	Porsche 935	199	–	–

Fastest lap: Jordan, 1m26.02s (122.71mph)

Class wins:
- Over 2000cc: Schornstein/Grohs/Rohrl, 100.35mph
- Up to 2000cc: Lombardi/Francia, 97.81mph

Group wins:
- Group 6: Brunn/Jordan, 99.34mph
- Group 5: Schornstein/Grohs/Rohrl, 100.35mph
- Group 4: Peter Zbinden/Edi Kofel/Marco Vanoli (Porsche 924), 94.46mph

Endurance racing at Silverstone in the 1970s & 1980s

Group wins (continued)
IMSA GTX: Bell/O'Rourke/Hobbs, 99.44mph
IMSA GTO: Yoshida Terada/Win Percy (Mazda 253i), 95.00mph
IMSA GTU: M L Speer/Ray Ratcliff/Fred Stiff (Mazda RX7), 88.37mph

1982 Pace Petroleum 6-Hours, Sunday 16 May

Position	Drivers	Car	Laps	Distance	Average speed
1	Riccardo Patrese/Michele Alboreto	Lancia Martini	240	703.68 miles	117.20mph
2	Jacky Ickx/Derek Bell	Porsche 956	237	–	–
3	Jean-Michel Martin/Philippe Martin/Bob Wollek	Porsche 936C	231	–	–
4	Giorgio Francia/Duilio Truffo	Osella-BMW PA9	228	–	–
5	Henri Pescarolo/Gordon Spice	Rondeau-Cosworth DFL M382	227	–	–
6	Ray Mallock/Mike Salmon	Nimrod Aston Martin NRA/C2	227	–	–

Fastest lap Alboreto, 1m21.18s (130.02mph)
Group wins
Group C: Ickx/Bell, 115.81mph
Group B: no finishers
Group 6: Patrese/Alboreto, 117.20mph
Group 5: Jurgen Lassig/Edgar Doren (Porsche 935 K3), 105.14mph
Group 4: Jens Winther/Lars Viggo Larsen (BMW M1), 99.60mph
IMSA GTX: Gianpiero Moretti/Mauro Baldi (Porsche 935 78-81), 108.79mph
IMSA GTO: Tony Garcia/Albert Naon (BMW M1), 94.76mph

1983 Grand Prix International Silverstone 1000km, Sunday 8 May

Position	Drivers	Car	Laps	Time	Average speed
1	Derek Bell/Stefan Bellof	Porsche 956	212	5hr 2m 42.93s	123.20mph
2	Bob Wollek/Stefan Johansson	Porsche 956	212	–	–
3	Jan Lammers/Thierry Boutsen	Porsche 956	205	–	–
4	Jurgen Lassig/Axel Plankenhorn/Harald Grohs	Porsche 956	201	–	–
5	Alan Jones/Vern Schuppan	Porsche 956	201	–	–
6	Tony Dron/Richard Cleare	Kremer Porsche C-K5	197	–	–

Results

Fastest lap Riccardo Patrese (Lancia LC2), 1m18.39s (135.65mph) (record)
Group wins
- Group C: Bell/Bellof, 123.20mph
- Group C Junior: Martino Finotto/Carlo Facetti (Giannini Alba), 99.63mph
- Group B: Jens Winther/Lars Viggo Larsen (BMW M1), 98.06mph

1984 Grand Prix International 1000km, Sunday 13 May

Position	Drivers	Car	Laps	Time	Average speed
1	Jacky Ickx/Jochen Mass	Rothmans Porsche 956-83	212	5h 5m 21.20s	122.13mph
2	Klaus Ludwig/Henri Pescarolo	Porsche 956	210	–	–
3	Rupert Keegan/Guy Edwards	Porsche 956	207	–	–
4	Paulo Barilla/Mauro Baldi	Lancia LC2-84	206	–	–
5	Jonathan Palmer/Jan Lammers	Porsche 956	203	–	–
6	Franz Konrad/David Sutherland	Porsche 956	202	–	–

Fastest lap Mass, 1m16.76s (137.50mph) (record)
Group wins
- Group C1: Ickx/Mass, 122.13mph
- Group C2: Almo Coppelli/Marco Vanoli/Davide Pavia (Alba-Giannini 001), 107.92mph
- Group B: Edgar Doren/Walter Mertes (BMW M1), 97.65mph
- GTP: no finishers
- GTX: 'Victor'/Gianni Guidici/Gianni Mussato (Porsche 935), 114.25mph

1985 Silverstone 1000km, Sunday 12 May

Position	Drivers	Car	Laps	Time	Average speed
1	Jacky Ickx/Jochen Mass	Rothmans Porsche 962C	212	4h 54m 03.22s	126.83mph
2	Derek Bell/Hans Joachim Stuck	Rothmans Porsche 956/962C	211	–	–
3	Riccardo Patrese/Alessandro Nannini	Martini Lancia LC2-85	210	–	–
4	Manfred Winkelhock/Marc Surer	Kremer Porsche 962C	210	–	–
5	Jonathan Palmer/Jan Lammers	RLR Canon Porsche 956 GTi	207	–	–
6	Klaus Ludwig/Paulo Barilla/Paul Belmondo	Joest New Man Porsche 956B	206	–	–

Fastest lap Palmer, 1m15.96s (138.95mph)
Group wins
- Group C1: Ickx/Mass, 126.83mph
- Group C2: Ray Mallock/Mike Wilds (Ecosse-Ford C2/85), 115.43mph

Endurance racing at Silverstone in the 1970s & 1980s

1986 Kouros 1000km, Monday 5 May

Position	Drivers	Car	Laps	Time	Average speed
1	Derek Warwick/Eddie Cheever	TWR Silk Cut Jaguar XJR-6	212	4h 48m 55.37s	129.08mph
2	Derek Bell/Hans Joachim Stuck	Rothmans Porsche 962C	210	–	–
3	Jo Gartner/Tiff Needell	Kremer Porsche 962	207	–	–
4	James Weaver/Klaus Neidzwiedz	RLR Liqui-Moli Porsche 956 GTi	206	–	–
5	Emilio de Villota/Fermin Velez	JFR Danone Porsche 956B	206	–	–
6	George Follmer/John Morton/Paulo Barilla	Joest Taka-Q Porsche 956B	205	–	–

Fastest lap Andrea de Cesaris (Martini Lancia LC2-86), 1m13.95s (142.73mph) (record)
Group wins
    Group C1: Warwick/Cheever, 129.08mph
    Group C2: Ray Bellm/Gordon Spice (Listerine Spice-Fierro SC86C), 116.33mph
    GTP: Yoshimi Katayama/Yojiro Terada (Lucky Strike Mazda 757), 117.79mph

1987 Autoglass 1000km, Sunday 10 May

Position	Drivers	Car	Laps	Time	Average speed
1	Eddie Cheever/Raul Boesel	TWR Silk Cut Jaguar XJR-8	210	5h 03m 06.22s	123.42mph
2	Jan Lammers/John Watson	TWR Silk Cut Jaguar XJR-8	210	–	–
3	Han-Joachim Stuck/Derek Bell	Autoglass/Shell Porsche 962	209	–	–
4	Jochen Mass/Bob Wollek	Rothmans Porsche 962	202	–	–
5	Walter Brun/Uwe Schaeffer	Brun FAT Porsche 962	200	–	–
6	Ray Mallock/David Leslie	Swiftair Ecosse-Cosworth C286	191	–	–

Fastest lap Cheever, 1m18.12s (136.82mph) (record)
Group wins
    Group C1: Cheever/Boesel, 123.42mph
    Group C2: Mallock/Leslie, 112.18mph
    GTP: James Weaver/Andrew Gilbert-Scott/Richard Cleare (March-Porsche 84G), 109.88mph

Results

1988 Autosport 1000km, Sunday 8 May

Position	Drivers	Car	Laps	Time	Average speed
1	Eddie Cheever/Martin Brundle	TWR Silk Cut Jaguar XJR-9	210	4h 50m 48.59s	128.63mph
2	Jean-Louis Schlesser/Jochen Mass	AEG Olympia Sauber-Mercedes C9-88	210	–	–
3	Mauro Baldi/James Weaver	AEG Olympia Sauber-Mercedes C9-88	208	–	–
DQ	Derek Bell/Tiff Needell	RLR Porsche 962 GTi	205	–	–
R	Jan Lammers/Johnny Dumfries	TWR Silk Cut Jaguar XJR-9	204	–	–
4	Bob Wollek/Philippe Streiff/David Hobbs	Joest Blaupunkt Porsche 962	201	–	–
5	Frank Jelinski/Stanley Dickens/'John Winter'	Joest Blaupunkt Porsche 962	198	–	–
6	Thorkild Thyrring/Almo Coppelli	BP Angelantoni Spice-Cosworth SE88C	191	–	–

Fastest lap Baldi, 1m18.24s (136.61mph)

Group wins
Group C1: Cheever/Brundle, 128.63mph
Group C2: Thyrring/Coppelli, 116.96mph
GTP: David Kennedy/Yojiro Terada/Yoshimi Katayama (Mazdaspeed Mazda 767C), 113.46mph

More *Those were the days ...* titles from Veloce Publishing –

Two volumes covering Brands Hatch in its '70s and '80s heyday. Both feature many previously unpublished photographs, and offer a very personal account of visits to the world's busiest motor racing circuit during two decades of excitement and change, both on and off the track. An affectionate picture of motor racing at its very best, recreating the atmosphere at the track.

£12.99/£14.99
ISBN: 978-1-90478-806-5/ 978-1-84584-214-7

For more info on Veloce titles, visit our website at www.veloce.co.uk
email info@veloce.co.uk • tel: +44 (0)1305 260068 • prices subject to change • p+p extra

More *Those were the days ...* titles from Veloce Publishing –

Oulton Park was one of the last circuits to play host to non-championship Formula 1 races. Set in beautiful Cheshire parkland, it was a favourite with the celebrated drivers of the era, and with spectators who could watch their heroes compete on a true road circuit. These books capture the excitement of racing at Oulton Park, and feature many previously unpublished colour and black & white photographs.

£12.99
ISBN: 978-1-84584-038-9/ 978-1-84584-164-5

For more info on Veloce titles, visit our website at www.veloce.co.uk
email info@veloce.co.uk • tel: +44 (0)1305 260068 • prices subject to change • p+p extra

More *Those were the days ...* titles from Veloce Publishing –

Superprix
The Story of Birmingham's Motor Race

The story of Birmingham's very own road race, which ran from 1986 to 1990. Featuring many previously unpublished photographs, plus drivers' recollections of the races.

£14.99
ISBN: 978-1-84584-242-0

For more info on Veloce titles, visit our website at www.veloce.co.uk
email info@veloce.co.uk • tel: +44 (0)1305 260068 • prices subject to change • p+p extra

Index

Abbey Curve 7, 8, 40
ACR Longines 80 32, 38
ADA
 Cosworth 02 81
 Ford 01 58
Akin, Bob 39
Alba
 002 61
 Giannini 001 52, 56-58
Alboreto, Michele 32, 36, 45-48, 50-52
Alliot, Frederic 36
Alpina 9, 15
American Le Mans Series 6
Ashmore, Chris 62
Aston Martin
 Nimrod 49, 50, 53, 56
 V8 16, 25, 26
Autoglass 74
Autosport 45

Baldi, Mauro 46, 56, 61-63, 67, 75, 76, 80, 81, 83, 84
Ballabio, Fulvio 73
Barberio, Pasquale 78
Barilla, Paulo 56, 67, 68
Barth, Jurgen 33, 35, 30
Becketts Corner 7, 11, 61
Bell, Derek 10, 10, 21, 25, 43-45, 47-53, 56, 57, 61, 63, 67, 68, 70, 74, 75, 78, 80, 81, 83, 84
Bellem, Ray 63, 67, 71
Bellof, Stefan 50, 52, 53, 56, 57
Belmondo, Paul 67
Blaupunkt 80-82
BMW
 3.5 CSL 9-15
 320 26, 27, 29, 40
 320i 16, 17, 19, 21-23
 320T 18-21
 M1 37, 39-41, 43, 44
BOAC 1000km 5
Boesel, Raul 74-76, 78, 79
Boutinaud, Raymond 60
Boutsen, Thierry 52, 56, 58, 61, 62, 64
Brambilla, Vittorio 32, 34

Brancatelli, Gianfranco 68, 69, 70
Brands Hatch 5
British Airways 1000km 5
British Touring Car
 Championship 14, 15
Brooklands 7
Brundle, Martin 74, 80, 82, 83
Brun Motorsport 66, 71, 76, 78
Brun, Siegfried 33, 35, 38, 41, 44
Brun, Walter 61, 64, 71
Buckinghamshire 80
Bussi, Christian 36

Candy, Vivian 39
Canon 52, 56, 57, 61-63
Ceekar 83JI 62
Chapel Curve 7, 32
Cheever, Eddie 32, 39, 44, 68 70, 74, 75, 78-83
Chevalley, Andre 32, 38
Chevron B36 25-27
Clark, Peter 36
Class B 9
Class C 9
Club Corner 8, 33, 52
Club Straight 13
Cooper, John 40
Coppelli, Almo 57, 58, 83
Copse Corner 7, 8, 11, 57, 60, 74, 76, 80
Cosworth 25, 32, 48, 71, 78, 80, 81, 83
Cougar
 Ford C01B 56, 58
 Porsche C-12 68, 69
 Porsche C20 77
Courage, Yves 58, 69, 77
Craft, Chris 25, 27, 28

Datsun 16
de Cadenet, Alain 25-27, 31, 32, 34, 41, 58
de Cadenet Le Mans 25, 26, 29, 32-34, 36, 41
de Cesaris, Andrea 68-70
de Villota, Emilio 40, 42, 46

Dickens, Stanley 65, 80, 81, 83
Dodd-Noble, Tom 58, 81
Dome Zero RL 5, 25, 27-29
Donington Park 6, 7
Doren, Edgar 25, 27, 29, 31, 40
Down, Richard 35
Drees, Klaus 20
Dumfries, Johnny 80, 83
Dunlop 52

Earle, Steve 66
Ecosse
 Cosworth C286 76, 78
 Ford C2/85 61, 62, 64, 67
Edwards, Guy 32, 33, 39, 42, 45, 46, 48, 57, 58, 60, 66
EMKA 43
Essex Petroleum 24, 30
European Endurance
 Championship for Drivers 50
Evans, John 28
Evertz, Egon 9, 13, 14

Fabi, Teo 45, 47, 50, 52
Facetti, Carlo 17, 45, 52, 56
Faure, Nick 36
Finotto, Martino 11, 13, 17, 45, 52, 56
Fitzpatrick, John 11-16, 18, 19, 21, 22, 24, 26, 27, 31-33, 50
Follmer, George 68, 70
Ford
 C100 45-47, 49
 Capri 15, 16, 18
 Escort 9, 11, 16
 Formula Ford 80
Francia, Giorgio 39, 42, 44
Franey, Mike 20

Gaillard, Patrick 32, 38
Galvin, Mark 65
Gartner, Jo 62, 68, 70, 73
Gebhardt Ford JC843 61, 65
Gelo Racing 16, 18, 19, 21, 22, 24-27, 29
German Sports Car
 Championship 6
Ghinzani, Piercarlo 45-47, 50-52
Grand Prix International 52, 53
Grano, Umberto 11
Grid Plaza S-1 45
Grohs, Harald 9, 11, 15, 21-23, 38, 39, 41, 44, 80
Group 1 18
Group 2 18
Group 3 18
Group 4 18, 35, 45
Group 5 9, 18, 24, 32, 44, 45
Group 6 9, 24, 25, 32, 36, 42, 45, 48
Group B 50, 56, 60
Group C 5, 45, 48, 50
Group C1 56, 61, 74
Group C2 56-58, 61, 62, 64, 65, 67, 71, 74, 78, 80, 81, 83
Group C Junior 50, 52, 56
Guerin, Jacques 36
Guinant, Gilles 60

Haldi, Claude 19
Hamilton, Robin 25
Hanger Straight 7, 15
Harrower, Ian 58, 65
Hermetite Racing 11-14
Heyer, Hans 9, 10, 14, 15, 18, 21, 22, 24, 27, 31, 39, 40, 41, 45, 54
Hezemans, Toine 16 18, 20-22
Hobbs, David 43, 44, 46, 56-58, 80, 82, 83
Hotz, Markus 19, 22

Ibec 39
Ickx, Jacky 9, 11, 13, 14-18, 21, 22, 24, 45-50, 52, 56-58, 61-63, 67
IMSA GTO 43, 45
IMSA GTP 56, 71, 82
IMSA GTX 43, 45, 46, 56

Jacobsen, Laurence 25, 26
Jägermeister 72
Jaguar 5, 74
 XJR-6 68-70, 72
 XJR-8 74-79

 XJR-8LM 74, 75
 XJR-9 80-83
 XJS 80
Jarama 74
Jelinski, Frank 72, 80, 81, 83
Jerez 74
Joest Racing 42, 46, 54, 56, 61, 68, 80-82
Joest, Reinhold 39, 42
Johansson, Stefan 50-52, 54
John Fitzpatrick Racing 66
Jolly Club 11, 17
Jones, Alan 52, 53
Jones, Richard 25, 28
Joosen, Eddy 21-23
Jordan, Eddie 41, 44

Katayama, Yoshimi 71, 80, 82
Keegan, Rupert 45, 48, 58, 60
Kelleners, Helmut 16, 17
Kennedy, David 65, 80, 82
Kinnunen, Leo 9, 11, 13-15
Konrad, Franz 22
Korten, Michael 37
Kottulinsky, Freddy 19, 21
Kouros 74, 75
Krebs, Albrecht 9, 12-14
Kremer
 C-K5 50
 Racing 9, 10, 16, 18, 21-23, 32, 33, 61, 68, 70, 73, 80
Kristofferson, Preban 27, 29

Lammers, Jan 52, 56, 57, 61-63, 67, 74-81
Lancia
 Beta Monte Carlo 26, 27, 32, 36, 39, 44
 LC2 50-52
 LC2-84 56, 57
 LC2-85 61-63, 67
 LC2-86 68, 69, 72
 Martini 45-48
Larrauri, Oscar 56, 61, 66, 67, 70, 78
Lassig, Jurgen 40, 73
Le Mans 24-Hours 5, 24, 30, 56, 73

Endurance racing at Silverstone in the 1970s & 1980s

Le Mans Endurance Series 6
Leslie, David 78
Liqui Moli 75, 76
Lola 56
  T297 36
  T600 39, 40-42
  T610C 45, 46, 48
Lombardi, Lella 32, 34, 39, 42, 44
Loos, George 31
Lopez, Manuel 66
Los, Costos 80
Lotus
  Elan 18, 28
  Esprit 26
Lovett, Peter 39, 52
Ludwig, Klaus 18, 19, 21, 45, 46, 49, 56, 58, 61, 62, 67
Luffield Abbey 7
Luffield Abbey Farm 7

Maggots 7
Maggots Moor 7
Mallock, Ray 49, 53, 63, 64, 67, 78
March BMW M1 37
Marlboro 50, 51, 54
Martini Porsche 9-11, 13, 14, 16, 17, 19-21, 24
Martin, Jean-Michel 41, 45-47
Martin, Philippe 41, 45-47
Maserati 8
Mason, Nick 36
Mass, Jochen 9, 13-19, 21, 22, 24, 27, 29-31, 39, 42, 50, 52, 56, 57, 61, 63, 67, 68, 74, 75, 80, 83
Mazda
  RX3 9
  253i 43, 44
  717C 50, 52
  737C 61, 65
  757 71
  767C 80, 82
Meccarillos Racing 19
Mercer, David 71
Merl, Volkert 22, 39, 42, 54
MGB GT V8 9, 11
Migault, Francois 25-27
'Moby Dick' 5, 18, 20, 24
Monza 63, 74
Moore, Patrick 7

Moretti, Gianpiero 46
Morgan Plus 8 35
Morton, John 68

Nannini, Alessandro 61-63, 67-70, 72
Needell, Tiff 39, 68, 70, 80, 83, 84
Neve, Patrick 37
Neville, Bob 11
New Man 54, 56
Nielsen, John 74-76
Nilsson, Gunnar 9, 13
Nimrod Aston Martin 49, 50, 53, 56
Nissen, Kris 80
Northamptonshire 80

Obermaier 73
O'Rourke, Steve 43, 44
Osella-BMW
  PA8 32, 34
  PA9 39, 42, 44
  PA9/82 45

Palmer, Jonathan 56, 57, 61-63, 67, 75, 76
Parc fermé 5, 31, 49, 55, 67, 73
Patrese, Riccardo 26, 32, 33, 39, 44, 45, 47, 48, 50, 52, 56, 57, 61, 63, 67
Paul, John 36
Pavia, Davide 57, 58
Payne, Max 28, 62
Percy, Win 43, 44
Pescarolo, Henri 18, 19, 21-23, 45-47, 56, 58, 74, 75
Peterson, Ronnie 9, 11, 13, 16-21
Pit road walkabout 10, 20, 45, 46
Plankenhorn, Axel 32
Pool, Colin 81
Porsche 12-15
  908/3 33-36, 41, 44
  908/80 39
  911SC 37
  924 18
  928S 60
  930 55
  934 16, 18, 26, 36
  935 5, 9, 11, 13, 18-20, 22, 24-27, 29, 31, 38-41, 44
  935-77 16-18
  935-77A 21-23
  935-78 18, 20, 21, 24
  935-78-81 46
  935-K3/80 32, 33, 36
  936 24, 29-31
  936C 45-47
  956 45, 47-54, 59-61, 72, 73
  956-83 56
  956B 61, 66, 67, 70
  956 GTi 61, 62
  962/962C 61, 63, 64, 67, 68, 70, 73-76, 78, 80-83
  962GTi 75, 76, 80, 84
  Carrera RSR 9, 14, 16, 26
Posey, Sam 9
Preece, David 25

Quester, Dieter 9, 11-14

RAC Club 7
RAC Grand Prix 8
RAF 17th Operational Training Unit 7
Rahal, Bobby 39
Randaccio, Ranieri 78
Redman, Brian 24, 27, 29, 30, 36
Regout, Herve 77
Renault, Philippe 60
Richard Lloyd Racing (RLR) 56, 62, 80, 84
Rohrl, Walte 26, 32, 36, 39, 41, 44
Rondeau M382C 45-47
Rothmans 45, 47-51, 53, 56, 61-63, 67, 68, 70, 75
Rousselot, Pierre-Francois 68, 69
Royal Automobile Club 7

Salmon, Mike 49, 53
Sauber
  Mercedes C8 70
  Mercedes C9 74, 75
  Mercedes C9-88 80, 81, 83, 84
  SHS C6 45, 46
Schanche, Martin 65
Schiller, Bernd 55
Schlesser, Jean-Louis 68-70,
80, 81, 83
Schnitzer 9, 12
Schornstein, Dieter 22, 25, 27, 29, 31, 38, 39, 41, 44
Schuppan, Vern 52, 53
Schurti, Manfred 11, 25, 27
Seagrave, Henry 8
Seaman, Dick 8
Sehcar 56
Sekurit 25, 29
Seven Copses Wood 7
Shell 74
Sigala, Massimo 56, 66, 67, 76
Silk Cut 68, 72, 74, 75, 77, 79
Silverstone 6-Hours 9, 24
Skoal Bandit 56, 58, 60
Smith, Robin 25-27
Sorga Racing 54
Sotty, Bruno 78
Spice
  Cosworth SC86C 71
  Cosworth SE86C 74, 78
  Cosworth SE87C 80
  Cosworth SE88C 83
  Tiga GC85 61, 63, 67
Spice, Gordon 25, 27, 28, 45-47, 63, 67, 71, 74, 78
Stapleton, Bill 35
Steckkonig, Gunther 55
'Stingbrace' 81
Stommelen, Rolf 16, 17
Stowe Corner 7, 29, 33, 62, 66
Stowe School 7
Strandell-Porsche 65
Streiff, Philippe 80, 82, 83
Stuck, Hans 18-21, 39, 40, 41, 45, 61, 63, 67, 68, 70, 74-76, 78
Surer, Marc 61-63, 67
Swiftair 76, 78

Taft, Raymond 58
Taylor, Wayne 80
Team Gaggia 56
Terada, Yojiro 43, 44, 52, 65, 71, 80, 82
Thackwell, Mike 70, 74, 75
Thomas a Beckett Chapel 7
Thruxton 14, 15
Thyrring, Thorkild 83
Tiga GC85 61, 63, 67, 78
Torno 64, 76

Toyota Celica 9, 11
Trimmer, Tony 39
Trisconi, Francois 32, 38
TWR (Tom Walkinshaw Racing) 74

URD BMW C-83 71

Vanoli, Marco 57, 58
Vegla Racing 38, 44
Velez, Fermin 74, 78
Veninata, Vito 78
Viggo Larsen, Lars 40
Villoresi, Luigi 8

Walkinshaw, Tom 11-15
Warwick, Derek 68-70, 72
Watson, John 74,-78
Weaver, James 80, 83, 84
Wilds, Mike 37, 63, 64, 67
Williams, Barrie 37
Wilson, Desire 32-34, 36
Winkelhock, Manfred 45, 46, 49, 61, 67
'Winter, John' 22, 80, 81, 83
Winther, Jens 27, 29, 40, 71
Wollek, Bob 9-11, 13, 14, 16, 18, 19, 21-25, 27, 31, 45-47, 50, 52, 54, 56, 61, 63, 67, 68, 70, 74, 80, 81-83
Woodcote chicane 29, 36, 44, 40, 70, 72, 73
Woodcote Corner 5, 7, 8, 24, 29-31, 40, 50, 51, 57, 61, 68, 74
Woodcote Park 7
Wood, Dudley 40, 66, 73
World Championship of Makes 32
World Championship of Manufacturers 9, 24, 45
World Endurance Challenge for Drivers 32
World Endurance Championship 61
World Endurance Championship for Manufacturers and Drivers 50
Worthington, Derek 11
Wykeham, Bill 35

Yates-Smith, Adrian 37